D1284878

Follow Me

The Disciple-making Strategy of Jesus

By
David E. Schroeder Ed.D.

To
BETZI
who has taught me much about discipleship
by living it
while I have written about it.

Many a woman
Shows how capable she is,
But you
Excel them all

TABLE OF CONTENTS

Acknowledgments

Some are authors by nature; others, like me, write primarily because they must, not because it comes easily or brings joy or satisfaction. Because this present book has been exhausting work, I have often asked myself, "Why must I?" Stewardship demanded my writing it! So many wonderful people have invested heavily in my own spiritual journey that I have been inwardly compelled to try to give a return on that investment.

The studies in Luke started in 1973 with a series called "What It Means to Follow Jesus," taught to the young people of Hillside Church in Armonk, New York. Thanks go to Dick and Diana Sylvester, whose enthusiasm and spiritual appetites as new Christians and youth sponsors encouraged me toward harder studying and deeper teaching.

In 1980 the discipleship teachings were given to the little church we pastored in Wokingham, England. There I learned that biblical discipleship is trans-cultural by watching proper English people apply the radical discipleship demands in a post-Christian society. Thank you, Browns, Dods, Mills, Margessons, Minors, and Redmonds.

The principles work well in a mission setting, as we found during a summer interim pastorate with Trans World Radio missionaries on the island of Bonaire in 1984. Morning sermons and evening discussions among several dozen mature believers helped develop the material more fully. Thank you TWR staff, Bonaire.

The writing began in earnest in 1987, when we began MasterWorks as a men's discipleship ministry. For thirty weeks, the Tuesday Morning Men's Fellowship listened to my teaching and worked through a big part of the *"Follow Me"* workbook. Thanks, guys. Members of the MasterWorks board have been so helpful. Over the years, the MasterWorks board has changed members, but the current board members have been most encouraging: Betzi Schroeder has kept finances in shape, Christine and Bryon Butler and Brian and Sheryl Schroeder have added insights, critique and encouragement, Shino John has literally taken the material around the world with me for use in many countries, and Keyla and Frankie Pavia have been recent catalysts in stimulating republication and new vistas of use of the *Follow Me* text and *Group Guide* in English and Spanish.

The *Follow Me* material, text and *Group Guide*, have been used internationally, and we are grateful to friends in Australia, UK, Nigeria, Zimbabwe, and Nicaragua for enthusiastically affirming that this approach to disciple-making is trans-cultural and effective. More recently, we have been using the material with Chinese missionaries-in-training in China and Thailand. And, a special word of thanks to the Cevallos family, pioneers of Programa BLEND in Pillar College: Rev. Francisco, Dr. Marcia, and Esteban, for encouragement and financial support to proceed with rewriting and publishing *"Sígueme,"* the Spanish version of *Follow Me*.

Elizabeth Schroeder, my wife and best friend, has been like a bond servant to me through this project. She postponed her own academic pursuits and spent tireless hours working on the mechanical aspects of the manuscripts. She has also sacrificed financial and material benefits as we braved the specter of unemployment while starting MasterWorks, the midwife of this book. She has endured with me the emotional waves that have nearly capsized this effort repeatedly. To her I owe the greatest gratitude, which I will attempt to display with a lifetime of love.

The originator of all biblical discipleship and disciple-making deserves not just acknowledgement and gratitude; Jesus Christ deserves all glory and honor for living the perfect life, dying the atoning death, and rising and ascending to our future glorification. He is the one who bids us "*Follow Me.*"

ABOUT THE AUTHOR

D r. David E. Schroeder is president of Pillar College, New Jersey's only evangelical, accredited college.

As president of Philadelphia Theological Seminary for three years, Nyack College and Alliance Theological Seminary for twelve years, and now Pillar College, Dr. Schroeder has been blessed to see healthy enrollment and spiritual growth in each institution. He has also served in missions with International Teams, Trans World Radio and The Christian and Missionary Alliance, under whom he was ordained in 1974, and served as a pastor for ten years. Serving the next generation within a context of spiritual renewal, ethnic diversity and Christ-centered higher education has been his passion for over thirty years.

Author of ten books, his most recent ones being, *Walking in Your Anointing*, and the sixth edition of the *Follow Me Group Guide*, Dr. Schroeder is not merely a theologian; he is constantly involved in discipling others. He and his wife Betzi have three married children and eight grandchildren.

Preface

On a Thursday morning the five of us sat in our usual booth at the Nautilus diner in Madison, New Jersey. Between bites of bagels and fried eggs, "sunny-side down," Scot, Stephen, Dave, Steve, and I discussed the morning's Bible lesson and how it confronted us. Through the smoke of the diner, one of us saw a somewhat familiar figure walking in, a new church attender who seemed to be our age. Should we invite him to join us? Our discipleship group had been together for over a year, but there was one more seat in the booth.

"Hi, there. I'm Stephen. Don't you attend the Chapel?" The rest of us were a bit surprised, but not displeased by our friend's overtures to the newcomer.

"Yes, my name's Rob. I've just come a few times but I enjoy it. Great messages."

"Well, all five of us go to the Chapel, and we have this breakfast Bible study every Thursday. Like to join us this morning?"

"Well, I suppose I could. Yeah, thanks, I'd like to. What are you studying?"

So it began – an unexpected odyssey for the six of us as the complexion of our group changed radically. Rob was a fairly new Christian who had received discipleship training while at college. Before many more eggs were scrambled or bagels were buttered for us over the next few weeks, we were in the middle of a group crisis. Rob's understanding of discipleship was quite different from ours. It was mostly sheer discipline, of almost military proportions. None of us doubted his sincerity, zeal, or ability to memorize scripture verses, which along with the daily "quiet time" was the essence of discipleship for Rob. But our approach seemed a bit less intense, focusing on relationships and character building. During the next year we would all learn much about discipleship, both through the scriptures and the challenge of getting along charitably.

Converts or Disciples?

The church's main job is not only to win converts, but to make disciples! I do not intend to raise the debate about the possibility or impossibility of being a Christian without being a disciple, but this topic is one of the most important issues in the Christian church today. The Great Commission (Matt. 28:19-20), which has been a primary impetus of the modern missionary movement, has been used with the heavy emphasis on the "Go." However, the real task of believers, including missionaries, is not to *go* but to *make disciples* as we move about in all the world.

Because of that clear command, it seems obvious that it is not possible to be an obedient Christian without being a disciple-maker. Yet this responsibility is not adequately stressed in the discipleship books I have read or reviewed. It seems that the end product that many have in mind is a well-informed, "cultured" churchman or churchwoman. Had that been the goal of Jesus, the Church would have died right in Jerusalem two thousand years ago.

For the most part, discipleship books travel on one of two roads. The more popular ones emphasize the gaining of rather rigid, external disciplines. Chapters are "how to's" on prayer, Bible study, witnessing, scripture memorizing, and good churchmanship, (attending, tithing, teaching, for example). Rob was steeped in this approach – but these were not what the early Twelve heard from Jesus on the hills of Galilee.

The other road taken by many discipleship books is a rough and rocky path usually shunned by all except those attracted to mystics, monks, pious hermits, celibates, those under holy vows, and communal Christians – in other words, super-religious folks who are somewhat detached from society as we know it. Those who travel this road tend to apply the most radical New Testament teachings without regard to cultural differences between the first century and the twenty-first.

With-ness

Thousands of discipleship groups have failed because they have adopted one of these two models – the ones found most readily on the shelves labeled "Discipleship" in Christian bookstores. Where making disciples *has* succeeded, books have not been in the foreground. Certainly the original Discipler did not put distance between himself and his followers by handing them a discipleship manual. No doubt he often used the Old Testament scriptures as he trained them, but his key strategy was merely to be with them. Scratch "merely" and replace it with "profoundly," for it was indeed a profound with-ness: "He appointed twelve – designating them apostles – *that they might be with him* and that he might send them out to preach" (Mark 3:14, italics added).

Being *with* a disciple is a prerequisite to making or becoming a disciple. No novice airplane pilot studies the flight manual and begins to "solo" immediately. He or she spends a certain number of hours soaring through clouds and landing in all kinds of situations *with* an instructor before taking flight alone.

As a young pastor deeply concerned about making disciples of the men in my church, I sensed that something was missing in the discipleship programs I had seen. The question that haunted me was, "How did

> The question that haunted me was, "How did Jesus do it?"

Jesus do it?" Is there enough information in the Gospels to discover how the Master Discipler achieved such success with his followers? I turned to the Gospel of Luke and circled the word *disciple* every time it occurred. Then I noticed large sections of teaching given by Jesus just to his disciples. Luke contains fifteen such sections. Most contain only one theme, although one section, Luke 6, has three. A few themes are found in more than one place.

Soon I noticed something very important – a truth that launched me into the eighteen-year study that resulted in this book: *Jesus taught character transformation.* All fifteen sections in which Jesus specifically taught his followers what it meant to be his disciple emphasize character qualities. He told them what to be like, not what to do. For example, the disciples wanted to learn to pray. Jesus gave them a pattern for prayer, and taught them a character quality: dependency. Although many Christians today know how to pray, few live dependently on the Lord. A parrot can learn how to pray, but learning to live dependently on God – eliminating anxiety, materialistic craving, and status seeking – is a far different story.

So, the biblical way of making disciples begins with establishing a good learning atmosphere with a disciple and a small group, and then focuses on the development of the inner qualities taught by and lived by Jesus Christ. This is the way Jesus made disciples. His invitation to Peter, Andrew, James, and John was not "Here, study the Book of Isaiah"; it was "Follow me." Please realize that studying this or any other book will not make you a disciple of Jesus Christ. This book, however, especially when used in context with other disciples, will lead you into the essential issues that

> These are the three stages in discipleship: learning kingdom values, learning kingdom ministry, and learning kingdom leadership.

Jesus emphasized and thereby provide the best environment for becoming a disciple and disciple-maker.

Another interesting fact I observed by studying Luke is the progression Jesus used as he trained his disciples. Today we read a lot about mentoring. Jesus took his followers through three stages of mentoring, which are seen in the three units of this book. In the early days he taught them kingdom (of God) values and modeled those qualities (Luke 5, 6). After they came to understand that he was the Messiah, they learned about character qualities that equipped them for kingdom ministry (Luke 9-12). Later, after he had told them several times that he was going to die and leave them, he taught them about kingdom leadership. These are the three stages in discipleship: learning kingdom values, learning kingdom ministry, and learning kingdom leadership. Each stage requires greater personal involvement between the disciple and the learner. Group participation also seemed to increase the longer the Twelve were together.

Group Discipleship

We need to be realistic. We need to recognize what Jesus knew: the radical hate, the vicious crime, the fierce fighting, the gross injustice, and the rampant ungodliness in the world and the human heart will not be challenged by a wimpish, fainthearted, superficial version of Christianity. The world needs to see virile, committed disciples, not passive, lukewarm pietists.

But what is a disciple? How will you know if you *are* one or are becoming one? Disciples of Jesus are those whose sole motivation is to be like their Master: "a student [disciple]... who is fully trained will be like his teacher" (Luke 6:40). "Be like Jesus? A lofty and worthy goal," you might say, "but unattainable!" True. But should that put us off? What baseball pitcher who ever threw a two-hitter was not trying for a perfect game? What golfer who ever hit a hole-in-one was only trying to stay out of the rough? What pilot who ever landed on the right runway at Logan Airport was simply trying to reach Boston? Becoming like Jesus is a lifelong pursuit. But don't despair. You don't become a disciple only when you have arrived; you are a disciple when you are earnestly on the way.

Becoming a disciple of Jesus does not have an easy, quick-fix formula. (Perhaps that is painfully obvious to you already.) So don't try to go it alone. You will need help – the help of God's Holy Spirit, giving you insight and power; the help of God's holy Word, giving you faith and direction; the help of God's holy family, giving you encouragement and making you accountable.

Many other Christians are on the road toward discipleship. To be sure, you are not in their shoes and they are not in yours, but you are all heading the same way. Your chances for success will be far greater if you work at discipleship in a group setting. One-on-one discipleship may have some benefits, but the fact that Jesus chose to use group interaction as his strategy should be a significant guideline.

This book has been written as the text for a discipleship strategy promoted by MasterWorks, Inc. Besides this text, MasterWorks provides a workbook called *The Follow Me Group Guide*. Our goal is to assist local churches in their efforts to help men and women exemplify the truth that *we are God's workmanship, created in Christ Jesus to do good works*... (Eph. 2:10).

The Follow Me Group Guide consists of three or four lessons for group use for each of the fifteen character qualities taught by Jesus in the Gospel of Luke. The workbook lessons are intended to be used in conjunction with this book's exposition and commentary on the fifteen passages in Luke. The best way to use this material, and thereby to develop as a disciple, is to form a small group of four to eight, have each one read each chapter of this book, and meet weekly to use the *Group Guide* to nudge one another into greater discipleship. A group of four to eight allows spiritual intimacy and gives the benefit of a variety of gifts and experiences.

The lessons of *The Follow Me Group Guide* are designed to help you apply the truth of God's Word and the principles Jesus taught his disciples. The questions are not threatening or complex, but neither are they simplistic. They will help you discover the extent of your maturity in each character quality and suggest ways to grow. Your group should proceed at a pace that is comfortable for all of

> A group of four to eight allows spiritual intimacy and gives the benefit of a variety of gifts and experiences.

you. The goal is not to complete the lessons, but to complete the disciples. Maturity, not material, should be your focus.

We also recommend that your group be same sex. Experience has taught convincingly that most men will not become spiritually open in a mixed group, as women do. The twenty pilot groups that "tested" the lessons found great benefit in the men-only approach. This is not to say that only men can be disciples, or that it is more important for men than women to become disciples, or that the principles in Scripture apply only to men. In fact, this book and *The Follow Me Group Guide* may profitably be used by women and in mixed groups.

For more information about *The Follow Me Group Guide* and MasterWorks, write to:

MasterWorks, Inc.
c/o David E. Schroeder
info@masterworksinc.org

PART ONE:

Learning Kingdom Values

Chapter 1

OBEYING ANYHOW: TEACHABILITY

Luke 5:1-11

Discipleship Principle #1
Disciples of Jesus Christ must be readily teachable, even to the point of obeying seemingly absurd commands that violate natural inclinations and reasonable logic.

I t was a cool, crisp morning there on the north shore of the Sea of Galilee. The distinct smell of the seaside – offensive to some, aromatic to others – left no doubt in anyone's mind that this was a fishing village. To confirm that notion, along the shore were small groups of men washing their nets, cleaning fish, and securing their boats. It was the kind of scene predictable at that location almost any morning of the year.

But, on this particular morning, interest was aroused by an added feature. A young charismatic visitor was using the opportunity to speak to the folks of the fishing community about his perspective on God and Judaism. He reminded some of John the Baptist, though his message and demeanor were quite different. John was rough, ascetic, and uncompromising. This man, Jesus of Nazareth, was more amiable and very magnetic, but he, like John, had a different agenda for Judaism than its major leaders espoused. This Jesus kept referring to the kingdom of God, saying it was at hand and that everyone needed to repent.

He seemed to be more teacher than prophet, though his words could certainly sting you. His compassion was evident, and one suspected he was a patient and kind man. Just exactly what the man's mission was and why he was preaching here on the seashore early in the morning was quite puzzling. Nonetheless, it made for a welcome change of pace. He was so spellbinding as a speaker that the fishermen were quieting their families who came to greet them. Even busy marketers with their carts of wares and foods were pausing to listen. Little children were being sent to fetch mothers, uncles, aunts, and grandparents to hear the Nazarene. It was the beginning of an extraordinary day.

When the audience became a crowd, Jesus got into one of the boats and asked its owner to drop anchor a short distance from shore. Then he sat down and continued to teach with words that were eloquent, persuasive, and unusually authoritative. Finally, almost as though he didn't want to interrupt the commerce of a normal workday, he concluded his message and dismissed the crowd.

Those who lingered heard him say to Simon, the owner of the boat, "Put out into deep water, and let down the nets for a catch" (Luke 5:4). This would be interesting! Few people in Capernaum would ever try to tell Simon what to do, especially when it came to matters of fishing, and certainly not when he had been out on the sea all night and was tired and crabby because, obviously, he and his partners had caught no fish.

Yes, this might be a real showdown, for the stranger was stretching his authority too far. Folks along the sea weren't apt to be conciliatory to inlanders, especially those from Nazareth. Almost everyone considered Nazarenes to be a breed apart—independent of thought and contaminated by the foreign influences that passed by on the major trade route. And the local gossip-traders had already spread the word that this Jesus was a carpenter's son and that circumstances surrounding his birth were mysterious, to put it politely.

Unpleasant, Humiliating, Unreasonable

Think for a moment about the most *unpleasant routine* that is part of your life. Washing dishes? Mowing the lawn? Getting up in the morning? Changing the baby's diaper? Driving a hectic commute? Whatever it is, the task is probably made more unpleasant by the thought that doing it today does not bring relief; you face the same unsavory chore tomorrow and the next day, and the next. Now think of the most *humiliating moment* of your professional life—the moment you wanted to crawl through the proverbial hole in the floor. Introducing your new boss and forgetting his name? Taking a colleague to dinner and forgetting your wallet? Misreading an important blueprint or contract? Attending a formal event inappropriately dressed? Finally, think of the most *unreasonable request* anyone has ever made of you—that time when your righteous indignation rose to an all-time high. Work overtime on your birthday? Loan your new car to an in-law going on a trip? Share credit with a co-worker on an exhausting project you did alone? Care for the nursery while a great speaker is at church?

Now put all of these horrible elements together: a disagreeable routine being done amid professional embarrassment and the anger of a most unreasonable demand. Simon Peter the fisherman was facing just such a moment. Every morning, after fishing all night on the Sea of Galilee, Peter and his partners had the disgusting task of cleaning their nets. Weeds, shells, unkosher sea creatures, tangled ropes, and holes that needed repair made this job the bane of fishermen. To make matters worse, on this particular morning the net profit (sorry for the pun) was zero. Not one "keeper." Irritating and embarrassing, especially when someone Simon didn't know greeted him with a cheery,

"Good morning, Simon; how was the catch?" Then this young rabbi/carpenter (from Nazareth, no less) presumptuously says in front of a crowd of townsfolk, "Put out into deep water, and let down the nets for a catch."

Could things be worse? Not for the burly fisherman. Little did Peter know that from that least likely moment the path of his entire future was being decided. He began to respond naturally and politely, trying to keep the edge of irritation out of his voice, "Master, we've worked hard all night and haven't caught anything..." (v. 5). Implied in his answer was an appeal to Jesus to be reasonable and sympathetic. Only one thing was on Peter's mind—getting home to get some sleep. The thought of throwing the nets on board and heading out for some daytime fishing was repugnant. To a carpenter, fishing was recreation; to a fisherman it was nothing but hard work. Why couldn't this man at least wait until dusk when they would be heading out again? The key to Peter's response, and indeed to his whole future, was his response: "But because you say so, I will let down the nets." Though the young Galilean was a stranger, something about him beckoned Peter's submission. So he launched out onto the sea and into the life of discipleship, apostleship, martyrdom, and eternal glory.

> Little did Peter know that from that least likely moment the path of his entire future was being decided.

Ready and Available

What was it that Jesus saw in Peter that made him a candidate for recruitment? Physical charisma? Superior intelligence? Potential leadership? Flamboyant personality? All of these were part of the fisherman, but none of them endeared him to Jesus. The essential quality that Jesus recognized in Peter was *teachability*, the willingness, yes, the eagerness, to embrace new truths though they dismantle natural inclinations and prejudices. Peter's aptitude as a student would be tested time and time again. He often failed the impromptu quizzes of life, but not for lack of teachability.

Teachability is the most basic quality of any disciple; the word *disciple* literally means "learner," and is descriptive of people who are open to new input, not just on the theoretical level but also on the practical plane of daily living. In other words, teachable people are not hostile toward change. They are willing to grow.

Many people are good students in that they will eagerly absorb new facts and ideas that appeal to their minds. Fewer are good disciples, who must also embrace new truth that tampers with their will. It's one thing to expand my pool of knowledge; it's another thing to meddle with my motivations and lifestyle!

Imagine how often Peter must have been ready to leave Jesus. It was a rough life, "sleeping tough" under the stars and clouds and rain when he could have been home with his family. Most respectable Jews thought Peter and his friends were crazy to follow such an unorthodox rabbi. And certainly the teachings of Jesus were often so demanding, even distasteful, that they caused many others to leave his service. What kept Peter around?

Fish! No doubt Peter often had a flashback of the hundreds of silvery, shiny, slippery fish caught in his net that morning when Jesus came to preach in Capernaum. He could remember his fearful amazement as he told Jesus, "Go away from me, Lord; I am a sinful man!" But Jesus responded, "Don't be afraid; from now on you will catch men" (Luke 5:8, 10). And because that's what Peter was learning to do, he stayed with Jesus.

More importantly, Peter's response of obedience despite his natural inclination was the reason Jesus stayed with Peter. Disciples must be teachable. Like Peter, disciples often think they know better than the Master, but the telling feature of whether or not one will be a disciple is a response that says to the

Lord, "But because you say so, I will let down the nets [or whatever he commands]."

John MacArthur, pastor of Grace Community Church in Panorama City, California, is known for his skill at making disciples and training leaders. He has a simple formula for assessing whether a Christian is of elder caliber; he calls it PATH. Is the man Proven, Available, Teachable, and does he have a Heart for God? Notice the lack of concern for ability, personality, and pedigree.

> **Is the man Proven, Available, Teachable, and does he have a Heart for God?**

Like Jesus, MacArthur looks for the right raw material out of which to make a disciple. Peter passed three of the tests right there in the boat. He was *available*, despite his doubt and reluctance to go fishing again. He showed he was *teachable* when he allowed Jesus to have the final say, and he evidenced his *heart for God* by his humble response after the large catch.

In the next few years he would become a *proven* disciple and leader, qualified to admonish fellow elders – "shepherds of God's flock" – about these same qualities (see 1 Peter 5:1-4).

Soil Analysis

Why are some people teachable and others not? More importantly, how can you know whether you are teachable and, if you are not, how can you become more open to new ideas? All humans are by nature "learners." As children, the wonder and curiosity we had about our world were nearly insatiable. Even if we rarely admitted to enjoying school, we all delighted in new discoveries. In fact, our curiosity often got us into trouble.

But a funny thing happens on the way to adulthood: The seeds of knowledge sometimes fail to take root, as Jesus illustrated in the parable of the sower (Matthew 13:1-15; Mark 4:1-12; Luke 8:4-10). In that parable Jesus was explaining why the word of

God, the ripe seed, does not always bear fruit. The problem is in the soil.

Hardened Soil: Prejudice

Some seed falls onto a frequently used path that is too hard for the seed to penetrate. One of the three reasons people are unteachable is prejudice—their truth system is so tightly packed that it will not admit new ideas, insights, or possibilities. The determination to block out any information not already in our orb of belief will also block out the potential for growth. Prejudice is more complex than bigotry because it is committed to intolerant, biased convictions, and it is more unreasonable, rejecting any new concept without even considering its plausibility. Had Peter been unteachable on the shore of Galilee because of hardened beliefs, he would have told Jesus, "Sorry, no carpenter is going to tell me about fishing. I have nothing to learn from you."

In another episode of his life, we learn that Peter was hardened on the issue of Gentiles being part of the Christian family. Acts 10 tells that somewhat amusing story of how God three times broke through Peter's prejudice by giving him a vision of a sheet lowered from heaven and filled with all sorts of unkosher animal life, which a heavenly voice told Peter to "kill and eat." Steeped in his Jewish scruples, Peter recoiled and refused each time, only to hear the heavenly reply, "Do not call anything impure that God has made clean." Soon afterward, three messengers from the Gentile centurion Cornelius arrived to ask Peter to go with them to Caesarea to minister to Cornelius. His soil softened by the Holy Spirit, Peter welcomed the men, although no devout Jew would normally invite a Gentile into his house. Because Peter went with them the next day, Cornelius's household became the first Gentile Christians, the spiritual ancestors of millions of others.

After years of observing Christians whose prejudices make them unteachable, I am convinced that their blind dogmatism reflects an insecure faith. Because such Christians lack the confidence that God's truth is the *only* truth, they are afraid that admitting one unfamiliar idea will begin to break down the fortress of their established belief system. The strength of their entrenched views shields their uncertainty about what is truly important.

How does such a Christian become teachable again? Although some are so hardened it will take direct intervention by God to cultivate their soil, God will often use another Christian to open that person to new possibilities. The more mature Christian in this situation must be gentle, righteous, and very patient. The most effective way to overcome prejudice is to present a model of greater tolerance and secure faith. Jesus did this, no doubt, with Simon the Zealot, who had been hatefully entrenched in anti-Roman prejudice before he became a disciple. Paul had to be such a model to Jewish Christians who were insecure about abandoning the Mosaic rituals. Of the three reasons for unteach-ability, prejudice is probably the most difficult to overcome. If you are a discipler of others and are working with someone like this, buckle up for what may be a rough ride. But it's worth it! Maybe your disciple will become someone like Peter – mightily used by the Lord to reach people.

If you suspect that you are a hard-soiled Christian, here are two helpful suggestions. First, find a Christian you admire, someone who is secure in his or her faith and not argumentative. Ask him to consider working with you on your teachability by suggesting pointing out issues where you major on the minors. Next, carefully and diligently study the life of Jesus, particularly as he related to the Pharisees. What were their prejudices? How did Jesus address them? How are you like them? Which of your dearly held convictions are truly supported by scripture, not merely by inference or interpretation? All other beliefs are like weeds in a garden that steal nutrients from the true plants and strangle fruitfulness. Get rid of them! You will be delighted with the renewed fertility of your soul.

Rock Garden: Preferences

The second reason for a low teachability quotient is described by Jesus as rocky soil. The seed sprouts quickly enough, but the roots never fully develop. When the sun beats down on the tiny plants, they wither because they have no depth. This kind of soil is like those whose lives are cluttered with their own preferences; the rocks of pride and ambition are more important to them than fruitfulness. Oh, they may tolerate the seed for a while, but it will have to fit in among the rocks. Such people have little room in their hearts for the ways of God, which generally run contrary to our human inclinations.

Had Peter been unteachable because he valued his own preferences over God's, his first response after his enormous catch would have been opportunism, not contrition. He would have tried to get Jesus to go into the fishing business with him! Imagine the potential of having Jesus exercise his power for the profit of your business. Many Christians not only imagine such intervention; they earnestly pray for it. In this generation of selfism, what else should we expect, especially when Jesus is often marketed this way from the pulpits? When we Christians are taught that Jesus the King is on our side, we feel entitled to all the advantages of privileges of royalty. It is not surprising that we sometimes envision God as a permissive, indulgent father and become a church full of spoiled, demanding brats.

Actually, the situation Jesus was describing was not merely rocks mixed in soil, but huge boulders underlying a shallow layer of topsoil. Some people are unteachable because they haven't yet developed enough depth for truth to take root and flourish. This may not be a permanent problem. They may just need an infusion of spiritual additives to dissolve the rocky obstructions. The more they receive, the deeper their soil will become. During this process the discipler must shield the learner from the heat of the day, lest the sun scorch the young plants. Some people hear a spiritual truth that sounds outlandish to them because it doesn't relate to anything else in their experience or thought system. Rather than exploring deeper, they postpone dealing with that piece of truth, so it withers in the heat of daily life. An experienced discipler will provide a support system until the soil depends and the root can find its own nutrients.

If you are a believer young in the faith, it is very important that you integrate your Christian beliefs and values into the rest of your life. Mature faith is not an appendage to a Christian's thought life, world view, and lifestyle. It is not a comforting and protective overcoat that can be dragged out on Sundays and shed the rest of the week. Faith is central in a Christian's experiences. It is the fertilizer that enriches, nourishes, and gives life its meaning. But it must be mixed in with the soil, not stored in a plastic bag in the garage or basement of your life.

It may be that you will need to discover what rocks are keeping you spiritually shallow and hindering your growth. These rocks are your preferences: the people, possessions, or practices in your life that compete with the ways of God for your attention. They may be all right in themselves, but your affection for them may be out of proportion with their importance. They become your idols if God is no longer in first place in your life. Peter had an established identity as a fisherman and no doubt valued the tools of his trade. But how did he respond after Jesus called him to become a fisher of men? Peter and his companions "pulled their boats up on shore, left everything and followed him" (Luke 5:11).

It is important to note that—since fishing, boats, and nets are not evil—the first disciples were not forsaking some illicit, immoral business. Similarly, some of the preferences that block our teachability are good things in themselves, but the place they occupy in our life may be wrong. If they keep us spiritually shallow, they block the seed from putting down a deep root.

My friend Art was like this in his early Christian years. His preference was cars, especially trucks, and his long-standing career goal was to be a mechanical engineer. Even as a high school sophomore he had accumulated all the drafting paraphernalia he would need for his engineering courses in college. But God had a better idea. His plan was for Art to be a pastor. It must have been quite a challenge for Art and his parents to face such a radically changed agenda, but since Art was a disciple, there was no choice but obedience "anyhow." Art has found, like all faithful disciples, that there is no disappointment in such obedience. Initial reluctance is transformed into joy when we obey the Lord.

Thorny Issues: Preoccupations

The third reason people are often unteachable is also seen in Jesus' parable: thorn-infested terrain. The thorns, he said, are "the worries of this life and the deceitfulness of riches." They represent our preoccupations with material security and status. Such cares choke the seed by demanding all the energy and nutrients of the soil. Because they grow much faster than the sprouting seed, they eventually block out the light needed by the true plant.

Many Christians stop being teachable because they allow their lives to be filled with anxiety over their real or imagined burdens. The only growth they are interested in is financial and material. It may not be that they are greedy; they are just insecure with what they perceive to be their vulnerable economic situation. This happens to poor and rich alike because we all tend to

> Many Christians stop being teachable because they allow their lives to be filled with anxiety over their real or imagined burdens.

compare ourselves with the next social class up the ladder. Once we reach that rung, we are still looking up, and there are higher rungs to worry about. Our vulnerability is really not so much financial as it is social.

If you find yourself being choked by the thorns of worry, you can pull those weeds out of your soil with the Lord's help. He has volunteered to take those thorns upon himself by inviting all those who are weary and burdened to come to him for rest (Matthew 11:28). If you are yoked with Jesus, those heavy cares that choke out your joy and growth are carried by him. We might even extend the imagery and compare them to the thorns woven into the mock crown that he wore on the cross. As surely as our sins were carried to the cross to be executed, so were our thorny anxieties. But unless we appropriate the truth of the cross, the thorns still infest our lives and we remain insecure and unteachable.

A practical way to handle anxieties is to list the tangible things that worry you. Then notice how many of them are vague, indefinite, or futile. One source studying this issue noted that of the things we worry about, 40 percent will never happen, 30 percent are over and past, 12 percent are needless health anxieties, 10 percent are petty miscellaneous ideas, and only 8 percent are legitimate concerns. And even the latter need not preoccupy you. Worry is a choice that you need not make. If you tear out those thorns and let the sun shine fully upon you, the light will make you a faithful, radiant person—and you will again be teachable.

Checking Your Teachability Quotient

How is *your* soul? Packed hard by *prejudice*? Shallow because of your personal *preferences*? Infested with the thorns of your *preoccupations*? Hardened, shallow, or impure soil will never yield a bountiful harvest. But soft, deep, and clean soil is the right ground for the seed of life to flourish and be fruitful. If your soil is fertile, you are a teachable disciple. Jesus told us God's will: "that you bear much fruit, showing yourselves to be my disciples" (John 15:8).

Discipleship Principle #1: Obeying Anyhow

The first kingdom quality is teachability. There is no discipleship without it. But this teachability is not the popular kind that fits a few self-improvement courses into a hectic schedule when it's convenient. Rather, it is an always-on-call readiness to learn in every situation, a willingness to be pushed out of our comfort zone, a radical obedience despite our natural inclination. Teachability is "obeying anyhow." It starts with "Master," and goes on to say, "because you say so, I will."

Discipleship Principle #1
Disciples of Jesus Christ must be readily teachable, even to the point of obeying seemingly absurd commands that violate natural inclinations and reasonable logic.

Chapter 2

WELCOMING NEWNESS: FLEXIBILITY

Luke 5:27-39

Discipleship Principle #2
Citizenship in the kingdom of God must be seen as an entirely new and unique life calling, not as something to be added to the old life.

W e do not normally think of Jesus as a party-goer. Church fellowships might have met his approval, but partying among sinners would seem inappropriate for him. Yet Jesus not only went to parties, he went as a celebrity invited by Levi, a later addition to the band of Jesus-followers. Levi was cut from a different stock than the rest of the disciples. As a tax collector, he was greatly hated by his own people, the Jews, who saw him as a traitor, a sell-out to the Roman authorities. Tax collectors earned their repugnant reputation not only by collecting the many irritating taxes demanded by Rome, but also by gross extortion. Since few Jewish citizens knew the exact Roman requirements, they were at the mercy of tax gatherers who usually took their not-so-fair share.

How strange, then, that Jesus would choose a tax collector to be one of the Twelve. Perhaps he realized that Levi, whom we know as Matthew, would write one of the world's most important documents, the Gospel that bears his name. Or perhaps Jesus knew that Matthew's presence would provide many opportunities to modify the anti-Rome passion of at least three other disciples: Simon the Zealot, and James and John, sons of a zealot. The zealots were committed to the overthrow of Roman rule, even by violence. Whatever the reason, when Jesus challenged Levi with "Follow me," the tax collector "got up, left everything and followed him" (Luke 5:28).

Life of the Party

To introduce his new Master to his fellow-sinner friends, Levi held a big reception for Jesus. Because there were all kinds of undesirables at this party, the Pharisees were looking on critically and grumbling, "Why would Jesus eat with tax-gatherers and sinners?" For Jesus this was a potentially dangerous situation. He was surrounded by two groups extremely antagonistic to one another—sinners on one hand, Pharisees on the other.

Why were the Pharisees even present in such a gathering? Understand that in Jewish society when receptions were given for a person of fame or significance, it was like an open house. Furthermore, some Pharisees had a devious fascination with the other elements of society. People who are self-righteous and outwardly legalistic are often extremely vulnerable to the sensationalism of sin. No doubt there was some of that in the life of the Pharisees. While they had very rigid standards, they did not have enough inner power to maintain pure hearts. They were titillated by the behavior of sinners, including tax-collectors and prostitutes.

No doubt the Pharisees were also curious about the man Jesus. They already knew he had done some rather remarkable things. But what did he have to do with this sinful element of society? When they began to criticize and to judge Jesus for being with such people, Jesus responded with this statement, "It is not the healthy who need a doctor, but the sick. I have not come to call the righteous, but sinners to repentance" (Luke 5:31).

Let's get it clear that Jesus was not here implying that the Pharisees were well. Chapter 23 of Matthew, in which we see that Jesus exposed Pharisaism with seven "woes," is ample proof of that. John 9 shows this plainly also. After Jesus healed a man who had been born blind, the response of the

> The only ones who will recover are those who confess their illness.

Pharisees was sharply critical because the healing had been done on the Sabbath. In the verbal exchange, Jesus' reference to spiritual blindness evoked the Pharisees' question, "What? Are we blind too?" The enigmatic response of Jesus was typically Hebraic, but its meaning was quite clear: "If you were blind, you would not be guilty of sin; but now that you claim you can see, your guilt remains" (John 9:41).

Quite obviously, the Pharisees were neither spiritually healthy nor righteous. But the worst part of their illness was their blindness to their condition. The logical deduction from this is that according to Jesus all humans are unhealthy and need a doctor. The only ones who will recover are those who confess their illness. They are the sinners whom Jesus came to call to repentance.

Which Prescription?

Before going further in exploring the next kingdom quality, let me interrupt with a very important question: What about *you* as a would-be disciple of Jesus? What are you doing about your disease, the sin that is hindering you from enjoying your relationship with God? People generally take one of five approaches to their spiritual illness. All these options are available to you, but only one prescription works.

First, you may *deny* your own disease. Like the Pharisees, you can tell yourself and others that you are perfectly healthy, that there is no spiritual illness in you. You certainly do not need a doctor if you are perfect just as you are. This prescription may also deny that the disease itself exists. This approach implies that we live in a utopian society free of impurities and that mankind is perfectly healthy. That is the position of today's secular humanists. It leaves no basis for morality or ethics.

As good as it sounds, denying the disease of sin has one basic problem—it is absolutely untrue, and we don't need a preacher to point that out. Every social commentator or observer with any insight knows that evil and immorality are not puritanical myths, but pervasive, infectious, and damning realities.

This was Jesus' theme in the parable of the Pharisee and the tax collector, told to those "who were confident of their own righteousness" (Luke 18:9). The Pharisee presumptuously and piously gave thanks to God "that I am not like all other men." He went on to list his religious credentials, while berating a repentant tax collector, who "would not even look up to heaven, but beat his breast and said, 'God, have mercy on me, a sinner.'" Jesus declared that the humble tax collector, not the Pharisee, went away justified before God.

A second response to your spiritual illness is to admit its existence, but *ignore* the need to treat it. This is the path taken by those who are too alert and honest to deny their sin, but find dealing with it is too painful, too humiliating. They would rather live in illness than reach out for help. Their major symptom is called pride, a reasonable response, perhaps, but only if they are willing to accept the consequence: spiritual death. Forever!

Spiritual death is the eternal consciousness and experience of the judgment of God. Part of being created in God's image is that we are eternal spirits. Our bodies will die, but, as both Plato and the apostle Paul affirmed, the physical world is not the essence of reality. Only the spiritual world is truly real. In other words, if you choose to ignore your sin, you will be eternally and painfully aware of your spiritual death. Because God will judge sin, if you allow sin to thrive in you, it will condemn you – a steep price to pay for your spiritual pride.

Third, you may try to *excuse* your disease by saying, "Well, everybody has it, so it's not so bad. And others have it even worse than I do." There is some truth to this, for everyone *is* a sinner and some probably sin worse than you do. Specific sins, by the way, are the overt symptoms of the internal disease: unrighteousness. By comparing yourself with others, you might take some comfort in not being too badly infected. This sounds reasonable, but only if you have a very inadequate view of God. His standard is perfection, absolute holiness, spiritual wholeness, with no trace of disease. All sin is to be eradicated, condemned. The heavenly Doctor is not satisfied unless all of this malignancy has been removed.

> Go ahead and excuse your sin, but then you must tolerate all sin. You know God won't do that!

The consequence of excusing your own disease is that you must then be condoning of all sin and be content with a disease-filled world. You probably would not tolerate all *sinners*, certainly not those who are the worst offenders – murderers, rapists, child molesters, drug dealers, and such. But you must give them the same privilege of excusing themselves and being intolerant only of those who by their definition are "worse" than they are. Go ahead and excuse your sin, but then you must tolerate *all* sin. You know God won't do that!

Fourth, you can try to *treat* your disease by yourself. You don't like the Doctor's prescribed remedy? Be your own physician. Try to eradicate your sin by your own efforts. Millions go this route. It's called "good works." Very admirable – but only if you are totally sure you will succeed in satisfying God with your efforts. And you never will. Remember, God's standard is perfection: total health, no sin. No self-medication will achieve that result.

The consequence of this do-it-yourself approach is a life of constant striving and agonizing uncertainty. Is it working? Did I do enough? Is God satisfied? What a terrible way to live! Why try to invent a remedy when a totally effective one with only pleasant side effects is available? The Great Physician, Jesus Christ, is God's remedy for sin. He has provided a fail-safe serum for perfect spiritual health—his blood—which leads us to the fifth and only worthwhile and effective treatment for your disease....

You can *repent* of it and undergo a spiritual transplant. First you must agree with God that your spirit is diseased, sinful. You must also admit that you cannot heal it and that you need an infusion of God's Spirit. God then places his Spirit within you by applying the blood of Jesus Christ. Your sin is removed! You have a clean bill of health spiritually and you are truly saved. The consequences of this method are fellowship with God, peace of mind, forgiveness of guilt, a cleansed conscience, a living Holy Spirit within, and the prospect of a productive life of service to God and to mankind.

Will there be any traces of your disease left? Yes and no. No, from God's point of view, in that he has dealt surgically with the cause of the problem "...as far as the east is from the west, so far has he removed our transgressions from us" (Psalm 103:12). But lingering symptoms remain, and we continue to sin. What do we require then? Another transplant? No, we already have God's healthy Holy Spirit within. The treatment is a fresh application of Christ's blood: "...the blood of Jesus, God's Son, purifies us from all sin....If we confess our sins, he is faithful and just and will forgive us...." (1 John 1:7, 9).

What will you do with your spiritual disease? Deny it? Ignore it? Excuse it? Treat it yourself? Or repent of it? Remember the

Great Physician's remedy: "It is not the healthy who need a doctor, but the sick, I have not come to call the righteous, but sinners to repentance" (Luke 5:31).

Back to the Party: The Parables

The Pharisees who were observing the festivities were not stupid. They knew they had better turn the conversation in another direction. When God's searchlight of conviction begins to get uncomfortable, most people back off. But not to be outdone, and still wanting to condemn Jesus for his flexible lifestyle, the Pharisees took another approach. They attacked the practices of Jesus' followers. Just like modern threatened unbelievers attack the church when confronted with the claims of Christ, the Pharisees said to Jesus, "John's disciples often fast and pray, and so do the disciples of the Pharisees, but yours go on eating and drinking" (Luke 5:33).

Jesus responded with three metaphors, or parables. One was about a bridegroom and his guests, which Jesus used to answer the question about fasting. Another referred to garments and patches. The third had to do with new wine and old wineskins. All three relate to the second kingdom quality: flexibility.

The Pharisees obviously approved the fasting and praying of John the Baptist's followers more than the feasting and partying of the disciples of Jesus. And wouldn't it be great to drive a wedge between the two groups, both of which were far too popular, as far as the Pharisees were concerned. Isn't it interesting how established religion can feel threatened by any different expression of spiritual life?

Both John and Jesus made the Pharisees uncomfortable, because John exposed their limited view of righteousness, and Jesus refuted their legalistic outlook on spirituality. John called for his own people to repent of their sins and be baptized, a very unusual expectation that no self-respecting Jew would submit to. John warned that it was especially the Pharisees who needed to repent and be baptized (Matthew 3:7ff). He would not endorse their complacency, couched in a religion defined only by rules. John demanded a change of heart demonstrated by the humbling experience of baptism.

Jesus was even more of a threat to the establishment. Whereas John the Baptist focused on the inadequacy of Pharisaic religion, Jesus destroyed its very foundation, the belief that legalistic performance would add up to righteousness. Both John and Jesus called for change. Rigid, super-religious people take to change like fish take to mountain climbing. They did not relish John's ascetic lifestyle and uncompromising call to repentance, but they abhorred even more Jesus' idea of principled freedom. In fact, they hated anything that meant they would have to change.

Do you know anyone like that? Do you see something like that in the mirror every morning? Most of us are somewhat inflexible, and the sad truth is, the older we get the more rigid we become. Our muscles become increasingly less bendable, but so does our will. We might call it hardening of the attitudes. Only God can help us here. Paul found the secret; he was pioneering into newness right up to his death. He said, "Though outwardly we are wasting away, yet inwardly we are being renewed day by day" (2 Cor. 4:16b). Daily renewal keeps us flexible, more willing to make positive changes in our mind-set and behavior.

To Fast or Feast

It is not surprising that the Pharisees criticized the disciples of Jesus for not fasting and praying properly. Inflexible as they were, they could see no compatibility between piety and partying. But is it possible that piety and partying are not mutually exclusive? Jesus' answer is neither simplistic nor legalistic. Instead, he demands maturity, flexibility, and sensitivity to what is appropriate for us at the moment.

Jesus again used an analogy to make his point: Should the guests of the bridegroom fast while the bridegroom is still with them? (Luke 5:34). No, of course they shouldn't. It is a time for joy and celebration. "But," he continued, "the time will come when the bridegroom will be taken from them; in those days they will fast" (v. 35).

What is our situation today? Is the bridegroom with us? Yes and no. Physically, no, he is not here as he was in the first century and as he will be when he comes a second time. Spiritually, yes, he is with us whenever two or more are gathered in his name. That is not the time for fasting, gloom, or sorrow, but for celebration, joy, and fellowship.

Generally, fasting is a private discipline; celebration is a public activity. There may be occasions when we are called to communal fasting and prayer. Those are exceptional times, and we need to be aware of them. But usually it is not a time for fasting when we are gathered with the people of God. Jesus talked about this when he pointed to the hypocrisy of the Pharisees:

> "Oh, you love to fast and make everybody know that you are fasting. You put on a miserable-looking face, so everyone will say, 'My, how spiritual they are.' You also love to call out your prayers, even prayers of repentance, in the middle of the marketplace so everybody can hear you. When you fast, you should keep it to yourself. Go home to your closet and do your mourning and repenting" (Matthew 6:5-6, paraphrased).

There are times for both fasting and feasting in the Christian life, but we need to be careful of our motives for doing them.

Problems with Patches

Flexibility means more than knowing when and how to fast or feast. Jesus also seized this opportunity to tell the Pharisees and his disciples not to expect his kingdom to be like a patch on a worn-out religious system (see Luke 5:38). His listeners clearly understood the metaphor.

The old "garment" refers to the Pharisaic life based on their interpretation of Mosaic Law. That law in its broadest sense was the core of Judaism. The new "patch" refers to the teaching about the kingdom of God. Jesus was saying, "What I have come to bring is not something you can just tack onto your existing system. It is neither an add-on to Judaism nor a new Jewish sect." The gospel is not a patch to sew onto the law; it is a new garment altogether.

It took time for that idea to become reality. For many years Christianity was considered to be an offshoot of Judaism, but eventually it began to expand into the Gentile world. Even then there was an ongoing problem with Jewish Christians who had accepted Jesus as the Messiah, but on *their* terms. They wanted him to be merely a patch they could apply to their ancient religious traditions.

The Judaizers, or Mosaic legalists, caused the problem that brought together the first church council. The question they faced was, "What conditions should be put on Gentiles who become Christians?" Should they not first undergo circumcision, the covenant sign of the people of God? Should they not first become Jewish proselytes before becoming Christians? The decision at the council at Jerusalem was that a Gentile Christian did *not* have to live by Jewish scruples (see Acts 15). Although the early church fathers prescribed a few regulations to moderate the behavior of the Gentile converts, their answer was a watershed mark in the history of Christianity.

Several New Testament books must be read against the backdrop of the Judaizer problem. For example, Paul on his first trip into southern Turkey, which was probably the province of Galatia, formed four or five churches. Right after the apostle left town, in marched an "evangelistic team" of Jewish Christians. Because they came to undermine Paul's gospel of freedom in Christ by teaching legalistic doctrine to the Galatian church,

Paul wrote to the Galatians and said, "If anybody is preaching to you a gospel other than what you accepted, let him be eternally condemned!" (Gal. 1:9).

Later in his letter he wrote: "You foolish Galatians! Who has bewitched you? ...Did you receive the Spirit by observing the law, or by believing what you heard?" (Galatians 3:1-2). Of course, the implied answer was "No." Paul here affirmed that further growth would not come by going back to the law, but by staying within the gospel of grace. In other words, early Christians were encouraged to put on the kingdom as an entirely new garment, not to cut a patch out of it to be sewn onto the old coat of Judaism.

The issue raised by Paul goes back to the confrontation between Jesus and the Pharisees recorded in Luke 5. There are, Jesus said, several problems with putting a new patch on an old garment. First, you will ruin the new garment. Just picture going into a classy men's shop, buying an expensive sports coat, and cutting a big hole out of the back so you can patch up one of your old jackets. Ridiculous.

Sometimes Christianity appears to be more patchwork than tailoring. It can happen on a personal level or a church level or a denominational level. We develop a patchwork faith whenever we eliminate certain features of Christianity that do not fit our style. If some aspects of Christian theology or experience do not make

> Sometimes Christianity appears to be more patchwork than tailoring.

sense to us intellectually, we spiritualize them. Or perhaps a biblical teaching is not convenient to our lifestyle, so we eliminate it or try to interpret it so that it suits us better. We abbreviate Christianity; we shrink it down from its fullness and sew on our patches in a design of our choosing.

The Christianity taught by Jesus must be taken in its entirety. We cannot buy into part of the gospel, choose the pieces we like, and attach them to our old garment. The call is for a radically new wardrobe. Jesus is not a patch for our old way of life. If we try to take him that way, we are doomed to failure. We are "turning to a different gospel—which is really no gospel at all..." (Gal. 1:6-7).

For example, if we accept "in my house are many mansions" without "take up your cross daily and follow me," we do not have the full gospel; we have something shallow, a poor substitute. Unfortunately, that is exactly what much of modern Christendom has done. Jesus saves, keeps, and satisfies. Praise God! Although we are glad to accept all these benefits, we rarely look at the fine print of his call to discipleship. Thus, the world sees self-satisfied and egocentric church people and turns off to Christianity. Nonbelievers who are looking for "reality"—a worldview worth living and dying for—will look right past the church if its members' value system, lifestyles, convictions, and commitments do not come up to the high standards of Christian theology. What this world desperately needs to see today is a biblical presentation of New Testament Christianity—the crown and the cross—lived out by kingdom people.

The second problem with putting a new patch onto an old garment is that the new will not match the old. Some people take a pet interest or ideology and try to weave the gospel into it. Christianity, plus. Many cults have been formed that way. Sometimes Christianity is a nearly invisible thread in a philosophical, political, social, moral, media, or commercial movement. It serves merely as the benediction, the blessing, sort of a lucky charm that is culturally acceptable. Examples of such watered-down Christianity abound. The "Christian" label has been attached to products and ideas as diverse as capitalism, Mormonism, cleaning products, rock concerts, home schooling, theme parks, nationalism, and plans to "earn an extra $25,000 in your spare time."

This polluted form of Christianity is odious and offensive to God. It is an abomination because it is opportunistic. Its purveyors are using Christianity for selfish motives, even if the cause is worthwhile in itself. All these defilers of the Christian faith are modern-day money changers and animal sellers in the temple of God and deserve the same angry response of Jesus: "Get these out of here! How dare you turn my Father's house into a market!" (John 2:16).

Another problem with sewing a new patch onto an old garment is mentioned in Matthew's account of this parable (Matt. 9:16). If we sew new fabric onto old material, the patch will shrink and pull away from the garment, making the defect even worse. True Christianity will never fit tightly with any other belief system. The kingdom lifestyle Jesus commands is always an alternative, never a complement. Repeatedly Jesus implied, "Either take my teaching, my lifestyle, my worldview, and my kingdom fully, or do not take any of it. Do not try to pull bits and pieces together to make up your own religion."

The imagery of garments is used frequently in Scripture to symbolize different principles. One New Testament idea is that believers will all go to a final Great Banquet. No Christian will want to go to that celebration in a patched-up garment. We need to be sure that we have discarded the old and put on fresh attire suitable for kingdom living. As the old spiritual song goes, we must "take off the old robe and put on the new." Christ is our clean robe of righteousness, not merely a patch of religion on a worn-out garment.

Soft Skins

The third parable about flexibility used the image of wineskins and wine. The symbols again are very appropriate. Because wine speaks of life, vitality, and transformation, it is often a symbol of the Holy Spirit in Scripture. What is Jesus saying here? Simply this – what you are receiving when you receive the kingdom is so new and dynamic that none of your old receptacles, none of your old structure and forms, are able to contain it.

Wineskins, of course, are made of leather, and new leather is very pliable. Old leather is rigid and cracks easily. Jesus was saying that the kingdom is like new wine – always in fermentation. In grape juice or other organic material, fermentation is a chemical reaction that causes expansion, which is why the cork on a wine bottle pops when first opened. If unfermented or "new" wine is poured into a new wineskin, the leather will expand to contain the fermented juice. On the other hand, if grape juice is poured into an old, rigid, inflexible wineskin and then ferments to become wine, the pressure from the released chemicals will cause the skins to leak, maybe even explode. Fermentation demands flexibility, or "soft skins."

Jesus was teaching here that people who want the new wine of the kingdom of God must be flexible. Kingdom life is too dynamic to be contained by rigid skins that it cannot shape. God's kingdom will not settle into the shape of any earthly mold. One absolutely essential quality we need for this new, life-changing gift is flexibility. Because church structures and dogmas can be quite rigid, it is often difficult for religious people to change. But Jesus said that if you are going to be a kingdom person, you must not expect to be able to use the "old wineskins" of your former life.

Three problems arise when putting the new wine of the kingdom into old wineskins. First, *the skins will burst*. They have weak spots that cannot withstand the pressure of fermentation. They have been stretched as far as possible and have become stiff. Many churches and denominations are examples of crumpled wineskins. They had hardened long ago, so when a renewal movement of God's Spirit came along, it was too potent for the old structures. A rupture took place and the new wine spilled out. What a pity! It is inevitable that real wineskins will harden, but not so with the church. Inflexibility is a choice, an attitude that can be changed. Far better to be supple and change shape than to be rigid and explode.

A second and related problem is that *the wine will run out and be wasted*. It will be gone, lost forever. No way of gathering it up again. If you try pouring the new wine of your renewed life into old, deteriorating wineskins, your new spiritual vitality will be wasted. The wine will run out through the cracks. Many renewed Christians have opted to stay within the old structures of their religious life. Those who do so out of comfort and complacency will lose their vitality. They will be diluted by the old wine and have very little impact on the church. Some, however, stay in the old wineskins out of concern for the church. They want to bring about change from within. This is admirable, but a caution must be raised. If you are a kingdom Christian, don't pour all your life into that rigid wineskin. Stay involved with a dynamic, flexible group of kingdom people who will encourage, renew, and support you in your discipleship.

Third, when new wine is poured into old wineskins, the *ruined* skins will not even be able to contain the old wine. This is why the old wineskin of traditional denominationalism is often threatened by the new wine of renewal. More than one church has been split apart by mixing new and old wine in old wineskins. Nothing good comes of this. Even the old wine, which may have elements worth saving, is spilled out. Traditional religion must seek to remain supple or it will forever be in danger of calcifying, cracking, and losing the old wine whenever fermenting influence appears.

We need soft skins for new wine. What is there about new wine that bursts the old wineskins? The chemical process of fermentation. As juice decomposes, it expands. Isn't that what we should experience in our Christian lives? First we decompose, or die to ourselves. Then an expansion, a vibrancy, a new energy that was totally unexpected, begins a transforming reaction in us. The question is, are the structures of our lives, our family, our church, and our nation able to handle the new wine? Or are new wineskins needed? Anyone who embraces Christianity without expecting its fermentation to alter his or her life has a surprise in store. If we are going to participate in kingdom living, we had better be flexible, ready to expand and grow, and willing to break out of our old forms.

Welcoming the New

Jesus ends this trio of metaphors with a curious statement, "And no one after drinking old wine wants the new, for he says, 'The old is better'" (Luke 5:39). Jesus spoke sarcastically here, as he sometimes did. Knowing human nature, he chided his listeners for being more comfortable with the old. The wine industry considers old wine to be

> Anyone who embraces Christianity without expecting its fermentation to alter his or her life has a surprise in store.

more valuable than a new vintage, and Jesus was not challenging that idea. Rather, he was making a point about human nature. The old and familiar status quo seems better to us because it is not threatening. The new demands change, so it seems safer to stick by our old system.

But what does God want for us as his people? He wants us to realize that new wineskins become old, just as new garments eventually become worn and tattered. Kingdom living is not a matter of patching up our old garments or even filling up one new wineskin and then just letting it be. God wants to be continually clothing us with new righteousness and filling us day by day. The Greek verb in Ephesians 5:18 – "be filled with the Spirit"—is in the present tense, indicating that this is an ongoing experience. Every day we must approach life as a new wineskin to be filled with God's new wine of dynamic fermenting, vibrant life.

The issue of gaining flexibility has a built-in paradox, a Catch-22. It demands flexibility to be willing to gain flexibility. This is an issue of the will, for human beings are not passive wineskins, destined to become rigid. David Mace in *How to Have a Happy Marriage* describes a study of people's ability to change. The conclusion is that we can change behavior almost

51

without limit when we are completely convinced that it is in our best interests to do so, regardless of our age!

Discipleship Principle #2: Welcoming Newness

Discipleship requires us to be flexible people who allow the fermentation of the kingdom to shape us rather than trying to impose our willful rigidity on the kingdom. The first disciples started their journey as rather stiff skins, but by watching the Master they soon learned Discipleship Principle #2:

Discipleship Principle #2
Citizenship in the kingdom of God must be seen as an entirely new and unique life calling, not as something to be added to the old life.

Chapter 3

REJOICING IN ADVERSITY: HUMILITY

Luke 6:30-36

Discipleship Principle #3
Disciples of Jesus are willing to accept and live by an economic, social, and moral value system that is contrary to the world's and to natural human inclinations.

After watching Jesus work several miracles, confound his critics, and woo the crowds, the Twelve were undoubtedly thrilled to have been chosen as disciples. They knew enough about disciples of rabbis to anticipate that they would soon be initiated into doing the same things he did. Imagine being able to attract a crowd by performing miracles, like changing water into wine! How satisfying it would be to silence the more educated critics with a cryptic comment like "Give to Caesar what is Caesar's, and to God what is God's" (Matt. 22:21). No doubt they thought that before long they would be healing the sick and raising the dead.

If the first disciples expected glory and public acclaim, they were shocked when Jesus took them aside shortly after calling them and began teaching them about the blessedness of adversity. Rather than filling them with visions of growing popularity, Jesus told them to be content in their humble circumstances, even to rejoice in their poverty, hunger, sorrow, and rejection.

Many modern-day disciples have had similar misunderstandings about following Jesus. Modern health-wealth-and-prosperity evangelists have assured many believers that as the King's Kids, Christians have a right to expect abundant blessings—financial, material, professional, and social. But the "blesseds" that Jesus gave to his disciples strike a different note altogether. The Beatitudes surely destroy any credibility that those who preach a materialistic gospel would claim.

The Sermon on the Mount represents the constitution of God's kingdom, and the Beatitudes form the preamble that sets before us the basics of kingdom living. If we expect to live in the presence of royalty, we need to know kingdom protocol, the attitudes and behavior

> He was not telling them how to be happy, but how to be disciples.

expected by the King. Jesus was not telling the Twelve how to add an extra bit of fulfillment to their lives. He was not telling them how to be happy, but how to be disciples. Blessings would accrue to those who understood and embodied kingdom principles.

The Beatitudes have often been considered "optional" teachings, specified for those who are willing to pay a high price for extra blessings – sort of like getting good seats at the ballpark if you are willing to pay a scalper's ticket price. This is an incorrect and unfortunate understanding of the Beatitudes. They are not an add-on reserved for a select group of particularly pious Christians. They are fundamental to Christian life and imperative for every believer.

Reverse Theology

You may have already perceived that Luke 6:20-26 sounds much like the Beatitudes found in the Sermon on the Mount as recorded by Matthew. Luke's account of this message is sometimes called the Sermon on the Plain because the text says Jesus "went down with them and stood on a level place." Despite its similarity to the parallel text in Matthew, Luke's version has at least two significant differences.

Careful comparison of Matthew 5:3-12 and Luke 6:20-26 reveals, first, that Matthew includes six beatitudes that Luke omits, and Luke supplies four "woes" that contrast with his "blesseds." Second, Luke's version focuses chiefly on economic and social concerns, while Matthew's seems more spiritually oriented. For example, in Luke it is the poor and hungry who are blessed, while in Matthew the terminology used is "the poor in spirit" and "those who hunger and thirst for righteousness."

Without doubt, the Beatitudes in the Gospel of Matthew are more frequently taught, probably because of the popular appeal of the Sermon on the Mount. And perhaps Luke's version seems too threatening to many of us First World, affluent Christians. Whereas the first disciples heard these teachings with great joy and relief, since they were already poor and hungry, many Christians today have never known deprivation, and many wonder whether they are excluded from the blessing. Indeed, Jesus was teaching his followers that in his kingdom rewards and responses to life situations are the reverse of the way they are in this world. Some have called this "the theology of reversal." A good example of this is Mary's Magnificat:

He has brought down rulers from their thrones
but has lifted up the humble.
He has filled the hungry with good things
but has sent the rich away empty. Luke 1:52-53

In the first century it was commonly assumed that the rich were under God's special blessing, and the poor were in his disfavor. Jesus turned that thinking inside out. He consistently taught that there is danger in being wealthy and that God has extraordinary concern for the less fortunate. For most of the world's citizens this is good news, but for middle and upper-class Christians in America this may pose a threat. If the rich, well-fed, laughing, and highly respected are to have the tables turned on them when Jesus ushers in the fullness of his kingdom, many of today's evangelicals may have second thoughts about praying "Thy kingdom come."

> If the rich, well-fed, laughing, and highly respected are to have the tables turned on them, many of today's evangelicals may have second thoughts about praying "Thy kingdom come."

The thrust here is not an appeal for you to live in guilt or to give away everything you have, go on welfare, reduce your calorie intake by half, stop laughing, and encourage people to reject you. Jesus gives no such command in this passage. Rather, he is telling his followers to place high value on their lowly estate, because if they are less concerned about their economic security, their social acceptability, and their reputation, they will be happier, fuller, and richer than if they are obsessed with these things. The focus of this passage is not on world hunger or poverty, although Jesus felt deeply the plight of the underprivileged, but on the individual disciples and their value system. For them to become kingdom people, they would need to appreciate their modest circumstances and place high value on the kingdom quality of humility.

Hermeneutical Fudging

Each of the discipleship passages in Luke contains one or more radical sayings that are clues to implementing the kingdom strategies of Jesus. When Christians accept these statements and incorporate them into their philosophy of life, a more genuine Christianity will be seen by the world. In the text of this chapter, the four blesseds and the four woes are examples of such sayings. To escape the "radical" dimension of passages like these, some ingenious theories of interpretation have been suggested. Let us examine three of them.

Some attempt a "spiritual" interpretation of Luke 6:20-26 that appears attractive because it seems to make Luke's version of the Beatitudes more consistent with Matthew's. We might easily say that Jesus was not really extolling the poverty-stricken, but the poor in spirit; that he was not talking about malnourished people, but about people who were hungry for righteousness. If we do that, we have taken editorial license with the Gospel of Luke, implying that we may continue to cut out of it other passages as we choose. This method of interpretation cannot be reconciled with a high view of biblical inspiration.

A second way of interpreting this passage is to "dispensationalize" it—to claim that this teaching was not meant for our era but for the *first* disciples only. This approach assumes that sections like the Sermon on the Mount were not given for the post-resurrection church but for the messianic community that preceded it, and that after Pentecost the Epistles set out revised guidelines for the Christian community. There are several damaging counters to this view. First, it was precisely *because* the early church lived out the radical sayings that Christians had such a phenomenal impact on their culture. Second, when we begin exempting ourselves from a command, where do we stop? What is to prohibit us from considering the Golden Rule, also found in the Sermon on the Mount, as merely a first-century dictum? If we consign "Do to others what you would have them do to you" (Matt. 7:12; cf. Luke 6:31) to just the first disciples, do we have *any* teaching from Jesus that applies to us today? It would certainly be strange for Jesus, who knew he was building a church that would continue through the ages, to give teaching for only the first generation! Finally, the ethical instruction in the

Gospels is the base upon which were built the moral teaching in the Epistles.

A third proposal for escaping the demanding implications of Jesus' radical saying is to "disciple-ize" them—that is, to apply them to full-time disciples only. This assumes that such teachings were given for only specially designated career Christians, such as the apostles. In this view, Jesus was not instructing "ordinary" Christians, but training those who intended to be more intense and serious about discipleship. Some have justified this view by appealing to a clergy/laity distinction that entitles nonprofessional believers to be exempt from the more rigorous demands placed on the clergy. However, such a dichotomy exists only to distinguish between functions in the church body, not to provide an ethical double standard! In the Gospels, Jesus expressed just one call: "Follow me." He did not call people to come first to get saved, and then later, if they were so motivated, to enroll in a discipleship program. "Whoever comes after me," he said, "must take up his cross daily and follow me."

I believe the correct way to interpret the radical teachings is to personalize them—to consider them applicable and binding on every believer. This is not to say, in the case of our text in Luke 6, that we should deliberately make ourselves poor. Nor must we try to become miserable so we can weep. Rather, it is to look at humanity through the eyes of Jesus and know that his values are very different from those of the world. Being rich, well-fed and/or highly celebrated does not automatically gain God's approval. By *his* standards, it is not society's heroes—sports stars, entertainers, multimillionaires, and politicians—who are "blessed." Some of them fail and fall in their lifetimes; and are to be pitied. Others have responded to the gospel call and been faithful servants, but it is not their earthly success that has endeared them to God. Although Jesus said to his disciples, "How hard it is for the rich to enter the kingdom of God!" he added, "...all things are possible with God" (Mark 10:23, 27).

Beatitude Attitudes

Agreeing that personalizing the Beatitudes is the correct way to interpret them, let us look more closely at what they say. If one word can capture their essence, it is "humility," a disposition toward life that holds values and priorities that are far higher and more worthy than the individual "rights" for which so many people constantly seem to be fighting. To show that Matthew's more spiritualized Beatitudes are consistent with Luke's, I will give an expository interpretation of the eight exemplary qualities found in Matthew 5:3-10. Careful study of the Greek words, reference to the historical/cultural setting, and comparison with other teachings of Jesus suggest that the disciples would have understood the Beatitudes listed in Matthew's Gospel this way:

To be *poor in spirit* is to have an outlook on life that usually attends the economically depressed: dependence, not self-sufficiency; social humility, not elitism or snobbery; frugality, not indulgence; and character transparency, not veneered sophistication. The "poor in spirit" are either the materially poor (as Luke suggests) or people who readily identify with those who are.

To *mourn* is to be grieved about a specific sorrowful condition or about the sad state of the world in general. For the follower of Jesus, such mourning begins with sorrow and repentance over the lack of one's own innocence and righteousness. Mourning is also the Christ-like response to all arenas of life where sin holds power and results in judgment and death. Luke's parallel teaching implies that this mourning often flows into weeping.

To be *meek* is to be gentle, mild, patient, and tenderhearted. The world literally means "domesticated," as applied to a wild animal being tamed for useful purposes. It calls for a quiet, willing, cheerful humility and submission to God, which stands in direct contrast to the stubborn, willful rebellion and self-assertiveness of the natural man. Meekness does not connote weakness or passivity, but active and voluntary compliance.

To *hunger and thirst for righteousness* may be interpreted as having powerful cravings that are either theological, as in justification; moral, as in personal behavior; or social, as in civil justice. The context indicates that social righteousness is Jesus' primary concern here. His people are those who seek man's liberation from sin's oppression, who promote the rights of others, and who work for justice in the law courts, integrity in business dealings, and honor in home and family affairs.

To be *merciful* is to empathize with others in their pains and problems. But it goes beyond feeling, since it requires the action of extending relief to the best of one's ability. The follower of Jesus is quick to see pain, misery, and distress and works to bring healing, comfort, and help. The merciful show compassion even when it is inconvenient.

To be *pure in heart* is to have simple, honest, sincere motivations. Nothing devious, ulterior, or base defiles the thoughts and will of the pure in heart. Their whole lives, public and private, are transparent before God and man. Hypocrisy and deceit are abhorrent to them, for they are without guile.

To be a *peacemaker* is to put one's own well-being, reputation, and life on the line to achieve reconciliation. The peacemaker is far more concerned about whole relationships than the petty issues that divide brother from brother. Rivalry, competitiveness, social distinctions, and self-advancement repel the peacemaker, who views God's family holistically.

To be *persecuted for the sake of righteousness* is to suffer personal indignity, ostracism, financial penalty or physical pain at the hands of those who cannot tolerate the example and reminders of righteous conduct. The blessedness of this rejection comes through knowing one is on the side of truth and has borne a faithful witness.

We should understand that when Jesus taught these particular attitudes of life, he was not singling out qualities that he admired in specific people. He was not saying, "John over there is gentle, and Peter hungers and thirsts for righteousness. Andrew is merciful, and James keeps a pure heart. You are really a good group because each of you has one of these qualities." That is not it at all. We dare not pat ourselves on the back if we find one or two of these qualities in our lives. Jesus wants every one of his followers to incarnate *all* these qualities, to embrace and exude the same joyful humility that characterized him. To be sure, that is a tall order, but it is the ultimate goal. Jesus says that a disciple "who is fully trained will be like his teacher" (Luke 6:40). Being like Jesus demands that we embody each of the Beatitudes, and the single quality of humility seems to embrace them all.

Blessings vs. Woes

Now let us look more carefully at the contrasts between Luke's "blesseds" and "woes."

Kingdom Comforts

The first blessing is upon the poor—theirs is the kingdom of God. But, woe to the rich, who already have their reward. This calls to mind the parable of the rich man and Lazarus, a beggar (Luke 16:19-25). The rich man was well-supplied, dressed well, ate well, and enjoyed a life of luxury. Outside his gate every day lay Lazarus, covered with sores and so hungry that he yearned for some crumbs from the rich man's table. Both men died. The poor man was carried away by the angels to Abraham's bosom, meaning heaven, and the rich man found himself in torment in Hades. Lifting up his eyes, he asked Abraham to send down Lazarus to dip the tip of his finger in the water to cool his tongue because he was in agony in the flames. But Abraham said, "Son, remember that in your lifetime you received your good things, while Lazarus received bad things, but now he is comforted here and you are in agony" (Luke 16:25).

Because most of us do not consider ourselves rich, we identify with Lazarus and the comforting expectation that we will escape Hades. However, we who live in First World countries, primarily the northern hemisphere and the West, certainly are the wealthier citizens of the earth. The very fact that we know how to read is evidence that we are among the world's more privileged people.

This idea came through clearly in *North/South, A Programme For Survival,* the 1980 report of the Independent Commission of International Development Issues:

> *The North including Eastern Europe has a quarter of the world's population and four-fifths of its income; the South including China has three billion people—three quarters of the world's population but living on one-fifth of the world's income.*[2]

Those facts may leave some of us totally unmoved, desensitized as we are by the frequent media coverage of famines in Africa, earthquakes in South America, tsunamis in the Far East, monsoons in the Indian subcontinent, and political and economic corruption in Africa, but it is undeniable that billions of people are Lazaruses, and we surely are rich in comparison.

> Jesus said that your neighbor is ... also a person of another ethnic background.

Let us also remember the parable of the Good Samaritan (Luke 10:25-37), in which Jesus told an expert in the law that loving one's neighbor is essential to being right with God. In the story, a Samaritan—hardly a respected member of establishment Judaism—is the hero because he was "the one who had mercy" on the unfortunate victim of muggers. This parable was told in response to the question, "Who is my neighbor?" Jesus said that your neighbor is not just someone who lives on your street or someone who needs help, but also a person of another ethnic background, and perhaps a different religion, such as a Samaritan was to the Jews. To be a good neighbor, therefore, we must humbly identify with the sorrowful plight, not only of others who are desperately in need of care, but also accept as a neighbor those who are not of our "tribe."

Well Fed, but Not Well Off

In Luke's second beatitude, the hungry are blessed and assured that they will be filled. The issue of world hunger can easily put us on a guilt trip. People have been dying of starvation for millennia. Our age is different only because that information is available in our newspapers and on television as part of the daily coverage of the world's woes. We need not accept personal responsibility for all the people who are hungry, since ultimately it is God's job to feed his creatures. God owns the cattle on a thousand hills and surely has enough beef for every person. Just as he multiplied loaves and fish during the ministry of Jesus, presumably he could do so again if world hunger were his *chief* concern.

Because of the horror of world hunger and mass starvation, we often lose perspective and mistakenly assume that first on God's agenda for humans should be keeping them physically nourished and healthy. But God's top priority in this world is feeding people spiritually. Although world evangelization must, therefore, take precedence over socio-economic issues, the boundaries between these two concerns greatly overlap. Effective evangelism ministers to the whole person. Since the growls of a hungry stomach can drown out the words of the gospel, part of our ministry as heralds of the Good News is feeding the poor. As stewards of God's resources, we must manage his assets with the same compassion we know he has. If we are hoarding and hogging what we should be sharing, we had better take seriously the warning, "Woe to you who are well fed now" (Luke 6:24). Referring to Matthew's parallel teaching, those who are not literally hungry should "hunger and thirst" for economic justice to abolish starvation and malnutrition in the world.

Manly Tears

Next, Jesus blesses those who are now weeping by telling them they will laugh. By way of contrast, those already laughing are warned that they will weep and mourn. Jesus did not say this because he was against fun, humor, and joy; rather, he was talking about an attitude of life. Matthew's parallel—"Blessed are those who mourn"—can help our understanding. Mourning here refers to feeling sorrow for sin and all its consequences. Laughing refers to taking lightly the effects of sin upon people and upon the world. Many people in our culture totally deny the concept of sin, and presumably they would be the laughers destined to experience "woe."

Some people feel cheated by this beatitude because they are not natural weepers. They may feel deeply about things, but their emotions do not come out through their tear ducts. Men, particularly, are culturally conditioned against weeping. But it is a fine thing to weep before the Lord! Jesus often felt and expressed great emotion. Looking upon Jerusalem and knowing the city would be destroyed in a few decades, he felt great sorrow and compassion. He openly wept at Lazarus's tomb, not because of the death of his friend (whom he would soon bring back to life), but more likely because of the fact of death and the way it devastates loved ones. Death is "the wages of sin" (Rom. 6:23), and the corrupting effect of sin on God's wonderful creation should cause all his people to mourn.

As a young man who found it impossible to cry openly, I prayed that God would give me the kind of heart that would at times move me to tears. He has answered, but not as I expected. At this point in my life I am not as likely to cry in sorrow as in gratitude. Thoughts of wonder and appreciation over what God has done for me, and certain songs that express those thoughts, readily move me to tears. Others find tears flowing in the midst of joy. Far from being considered a sign of weakness and lack of "masculinity," tears should be seen as evidence of deep caring. Crying itself is not an evidence of spiritual maturity, but the farther we go in our walk with God, the more likely we are to enter into the blessing of those who weep. Matthew's parallel teaching does not focus on weeping but on mourning. Tears do not commend us to God unless they flow out of a heart broken by the sorrows of others.

"Because of the Son of Man"

The fourth and last of Luke's beatitudes (Luke 6:22) is a blessing upon all who are hated, excluded, insulted, and rejected for the sake of Jesus. They are to rejoice and leap for joy because they have a great reward in heaven, like the true prophets of God, who also were abused for their faithfulness. They phrase "because of the Son of Man" is important here because the blessing is not promised simply for being unpopular. Our rejection must be because of our attachment to Jesus, not because of a negative personality trait, misconduct, or inability to befriend others. By way of contrast, the Luke passage warns against placing stock in the praises of men—"for that is how their fathers treated the false prophets" (v. 26).

Humility

Underlying all the Beatitudes is the kingdom quality of humility. If we crave ever-greater financial and social status, letting materialistic success symbols become obsessions to us, we will be of little value to the work of God's kingdom and be poor representatives of what the kingdom is all about. While poverty, hunger, weeping, and rejection may not be part of our life goals, neither should obtaining wealth, feasting lavishly, living as though life is always a party, and seeking popularity.

A big part of humility is contentment: rejoicing even in adversity. People of the kingdom are not self-strivers; they are not out to elevate their own status according to the values of the world. This is not to say that the poor and hungry should be happy *about* their poverty and starvation. Rather, disciples are to be content with the lowly status and reputation usually reserved for the poor and hungry. Social climbing is contrary to kingdom living. The only elevation Jesus sought was on the cross, and he bids us to follow him.

Sexual Values

At this point I will take a liberty and push beyond the explicit teaching of the text to state a further application that is important for every person's discipleship. I refer to our sexual values. If we are to be known as a people who bear the character imprint of God, our values will need to be transformed in the area of life with which our society is perilously obsessed: sex. The so-called sexual revolution has given us cultural standards that encourage all forms of carnal expression and implies that sexual activity is neither moral nor immoral, as long as no one gets hurt. Because many in the church have been swept into this heretical ideology, it must be addressed in any discussion about discipleship.

We have the Gentile Christians in Corinth to thank for raising issues that were not usually discussed publicly in Jewish society. Chapter 7 of Paul's first epistle to the Corinthians addresses several domestic and sexual questions that are still relevant today. Sexual responsibility in marriage, marriage between believer and unbeliever, divorce, abandonment, celibacy, and widowhood were among the issues needing clarification. Paul's basic guideline was that each believer should learn contentment. While certain liberties are affirmed, Paul taught that wisdom calls for self-control. A Christian "will not be mastered by anything," for we are to "honor God" with our bodies (1 Cor. 6:12, 20).

There is no doubt in my mind that in private moments Jesus instructed his disciples about their sexuality and how to harness it for holy purposes. He told them explicitly that lusting after a woman was as wrong as committing an adulterous act. His own relationships with women were so wholesome that the disciples were constantly seeing God's standard of purity being modeled.

Our society tolerates and encourages such excesses of sexual expression, experimentation, and exploitation that we easily become immune to what the movie industry calls "adult situations" in every branch of the media world. Richard Foster, in *Money, Sex & Power*, says we live in a "sex-soaked culture." It is not my purpose here to ask you to get on an anti-pornography bandwagon (although that is not a bad idea), but to have you see that you are constantly being bombarded with a message that says, "Sex is the ultimate experience, and as long as no one gets hurt, go for it." A more subtle part of the message is "Don't be content with what you have; seek greater thrills in the playground of sex." In a section called, "Distorted Sexuality," Foster writes:

> *The slick film, with its carefully packaged titillations, can make an otherwise wholesome marriage relationship seem tedious and drab by comparison. What woman can compare favorably day in and day out with the voluptuous breasts, sparkling smile, and sensuous legs seen on the screen today:...The answer is that no one can, not even the people who stage the phony show. It is a dream world—a deceptive, beguiling, artificial dream world....Such make-believe is genuinely destructive to both true sexuality and true spirituality.[3]*

If we are serious about discipleship, we will not physically wander outside the boundaries of biblically sanctioned sex. But the question each of us must face is: Have I submitted my sexuality to the Lord so that I will be content in my present situation even though the rest of the world is seducing me away from sexual holiness?

The people most at risk are those who travel frequently. Temptations quickly overruled at home have greater power on the road because of the availability of sensual opportunities that may seemingly be indulged in anonymity. Men who must travel for business purposes are wise to become accountable to other Christian men with whom they can be honest about these temptations. One discipleship group in a church I attended had an arrangement in which each man had to submit detailed travel itineraries to the others. It was not unusual for a traveler to receive a call in his hotel room late at night, asking what he had on the television, and whether he had watched any pay-per-view movie he would not view with his wife. This issue deserves open and honest discussion in a discipleship group. For many men, their sexual life is the cutting edge for them spiritually. Victory in that battle is key to the whole war.

Discipleship Principle #3: Rejoicing in Adversity

By following the pattern of Christ, we submit fully to God in every area of life and discover the blessedness of humility. That is exactly the thrust of Discipleship Principle #3:

Discipleship Principle #3
Disciples of Jesus are willing to accept and live by an economic, social, and moral value system that is contrary to the world's and to natural human inclinations.

Chapter 4

HANDLING REJECTION: COMPASSION

Luke 6:27-36

Discipleship Principle #4
In kingdom living, disciples of Jesus Christ respond to hostility and rejection by treating their enemies as well as they want to be treated themselves.

Peering into the future of his disciples' lives, Jesus could see storm clouds gathering. He knew that they would face much conflict and rejection. He also knew that being rejected would give them opportunities to show the difference between natural responses and kingdom responses. The natural response to hostility is either to run or to fight; in other words to react negatively to an "enemy." Kingdom living calls for a positive, compassionate commitment to those who reject you. This would be an expensive lesson for the disciples to learn. Some of them, including Jesus himself, would pay for the principle with their lives.

One of the sure clues that kingdom principles are generally not understood even by very intelligent people is the idea that

Christian faith is merely a crutch for those who are weak. Sigmund Freud, for instance, taught that belief in God is wish projection, whereby people who cannot tolerate being orphans in the universe hypothesize the existence of a super-Father with infinite attributes of love and strength. Freud implies that many believers are emotional cripples who need God as their psychological crutch. Truly mature humans, he suggests, cast aside all such superstitious props and fend for themselves in a naturalistic world.

Christianity of the Crutch

There is indeed a type of faith system in which God is used as a crutch, and it is probably the most popular brand of Christianity. If you look carefully through an old hymnal or at contemporary songs, you will find that many of the favorites emphasize safety, security, and dependency topics. Such songs as "Rock of Ages," "Leaning on the Everlasting Arms," "Under His Wings," "Never Let Me Go," "All I Need is You," and "Lord, I Need You" come quickly to mind. It is easy to see how a skeptic can say that Christianity is just for wimps who need propping up.

In reality, these songs express devotional richness and are greatly beneficial if mixed with emotional and spiritual maturity, but for many people Christianity is only a convenient tool, one way to achieve self-centered goals. Perhaps this is because a cheapened and distorted gospel is too often peddled. This simplistic Good News says: You are desperately in need of being saved; you will suffer eternal pain unless you pray to ask Jesus to come into your heart and to forgive you of your sins; if you repent, you will be happier in this life and receive eternal rewards in heaven. Sounds great, right? So you accept Jesus and are saved—but nothing has been said about discipleship. It is strictly a matter of how you can get the most good for yourself and avoid the most pain. Bonhoeffer called this "cheap grace."

That kind of gospel does not bother to let people in on the fine print of discipleship until after they sign on the dotted line. For some strange reason, many otherwise sincere Christians have the idea that people who are saved must then go through a trial period of several years to make sure they are really serious before they can be told about discipleship.

Jesus never did it that way. Jesus did not try to get people saved so that later he might recruit them to be disciples. His call to people was "Come, follow. Be my disciple right now." Some really wanted to come but only on their own terms. Jesus did not get on his knees and beg them to reconsider. Nor did he say, "I'll be here when you are ready." Rather, the implication was, "Sorry, friend, this business is of such urgency that all other issues, no matter how important they may seem to you, are of secondary importance."

This is the Jesus you see in the Gospels, and his kind of Christianity is not a crutch. In fact, it kicks all the props out from under you. Instead of crutches, Christ offers a cross. Today we call that brand of Christianity *radical* because there are so few examples of it. Yet Christianity of the cross made the first-century church successful, and the lack of that kind of commitment explains the impotence of the twenty-first century

> Jesus did not try to get people saved so that later on he might recruit them to be disciples.

church. Most of what today's church is doing well is related to its members' ability to fork out enough money to do "good works." Today's church cannot say, "Silver and gold I do not have," nor can it say, "Rise up and walk." Instead, its very generosity is presented as a crutch for staggering people.

Like Father, Like Son

Luke 6:27-38 follows the blessed and woes of the Beatitudes. Notice in verse 20 whom Jesus addressed with this teaching: "Looking at his disciples, he said...." The previous

71

verses indicate that there were many people around him, but he turned his attention to his disciples for this particular teaching. Jesus was concerned that his followers learn how to respond to rejection: They must love those who mistreat them. Because the lesson was a difficult one, Jesus gave the Twelve some extra motivation. In summing up the idea of compassionate response to enemies, Jesus said that then "...you will be sons of the Most High, because he is kind to the ungrateful and wicked" (v. 35).

In Genesis 1:27 we are told that God has created us in his image. Part of God's image is his character, and part of that character is his kindness to ungrateful and evil men. By living the way Jesus prescribed here, we affirm the image of God in ourselves. It ought to mean everything to us to accomplish what God wants us to do and become what God wants us to be. Unless we become and achieve those things that God expects, all other success is illusory.

Becoming godly in character and behavior must be our highest priority and a lifelong calling. If we sit back and refuse to be concerned about that goal, we fail as human beings because we are denying the image of God in which we are created. When we respond to rejection his way—with compassion—we are sons of the Most High—like Father, like son. Therefore, we must be merciful, just as our Father is merciful (v. 36).

The Responses

Now let us look more closely at what Jesus said about the way we are to respond to rejection. In this passage there are four categories of responses to four different kinds of rejection.

Love Whom?

First, Jesus assumed that his followers would have enemies, so he said, "But I tell you who hear me: Love your enemies..." (Luke 6:27). Jesus himself had enemies and still does. People who did not accept his teaching became his enemies, for no one could just walk away passively. His teaching and life always confronted people with options. His call was demanding, and many people knew inwardly that he was right, if for no other reason, than by the way he lived, which was a great credential for the truthfulness of his teaching. Those who would not accept the rigorous righteousness he taught were rejecting Jesus' claims and thereby became his enemies.

There are several passages in Scripture supporting the idea that Christians are likely to have enemies, such as, "...friendship with the world is hatred toward God" (James 4:4). We are enemies of God if we choose to be friends to the world. The converse is also true: If we become friends of God, some people in the world will become our enemies, just as they are God's enemies. Jesus does not want us deliberately to make enemies through obnoxious behavior or personality traits. (Many of us would have no trouble doing that!) Nevertheless, our stand for righteousness will always arouse hostility in people who are repelled by virtue. Because that will happen, Jesus commanded that his followers respond to enemies in one way – with love.

What is love? The Greek word *agape* means an unconditional love, a God-like love that is selfless and oriented totally toward the object of that love. It is an active expression, not just a feeling; an act of the will, not just an emotional response. Agape moves us to *do* something positive, although Jesus did not say exactly what to do. Situations differ and will determine the appropriate action, but our response to our enemies should be to do something "loving," which comes out of a genuine and compassionate heart.

How can you do that? Simply stated: by looking at your enemy through God's eyes. Do not respond, "I'm being attacked; I'm being hated." If you take it personally, you will want to retaliate or retreat. Identify so fully with God that when you look at that person through God's eyes, you will see someone who is probably alienated from God and may have reasons to feel insecure and threatened. There stands a person who is responding out of anxiety, who may not have the peace of God that you have ruling in your life, who may not know the forgiveness of sins, who does not have the hope of eternal life. That person may seem to be your enemy, but God loves him or her as much as he loves you. When we look at others through God's eyes, it is possible to respond in a loving way even to our enemies.

When your enemy is another member in the body of Christ, it is even more imperative to love that person. In his high priestly prayer shortly before his crucifixion (John 17), Jesus affirmed that to the watching world the sign of the reality and truthfulness of his teachings is the love among the brothers. When there is alienation, fragmentation, hostility, and enmity in the body of Christ, people in the world conclude that the way of Jesus is a fraud and a sham, not worth looking at twice. When the unity of the body of Christ breaks down because our relationship with another Christian is not loving, we are putting out a sign: "Do not come here; you will not find the kingdom of God here." Loving enemies must carry over into the community of believers.

You may say, "Okay, I can give my non-Christian enemy the benefit of the doubt. I'll try to see him through God's eyes and love him. But my Christian enemy has no excuse. What motivation can cause me to love him?" The answer is simple to grasp – exactly the same as for the unbeliever: Look at your Christian enemy through God's eyes. Your enemy in the church is part of God's workmanship (Eph. 2:10), a disciple in the making, just as you are. He may not be as far along as you, but he will get there if you and other Christians give him grace instead of judgment.

Some years ago many Christians wore a lapel pin with the letters PBPGINFWMY – "Please Be Patient; God Is Not Finished With Me Yet." This was an apt reminder that all of us are work in process, not finished goods. Galatians 6:10 tells us to "do good to all people, especially to those who belong to the family of believers." Why is it that some Christians are more patient with the Department of Transportation's snail-like efforts to repair the local highway than we are with God when he is building up another disciple? And it does come down to that, because by not responding in love to an unfinished disciple, we show impatience with God.

But He Hates Me!

The second response to rejection is to "do good to those who hate you" (Luke 6:27b). Again, Jesus is taking for granted that his followers will be hated by some. When Jesus spoke about the disciples' relation to the world, he said, "If the world hates you, keep in mind that it hated me first. If you belonged to the world, it would love you as its own. As it is, you do not belong to the world, but I have chosen you out of the world. That is why the world hates you" (John 15:18-19). But how are we to treat those who hate us? *Do good to them!* The sense of this phrase is to do good as a normal practice, not only when we feel hated.

Why did Jesus prescribe such an unreasonable response? It is part of the strategy of the kingdom. The world is not used to that kind of behavior. Our responding to hatred with good deeds, causes unbelievers to wake up, shake their heads and say, "What's going on? What kind of person is that? What's he made out of?" Undoubtedly that happened frequently in the first century. It still does occasionally. If exchanging good deeds for hatred were the normal response of all Christians, the world would be forced to see that the life Jesus prescribes is truly God-oriented and that Christianity is true.

Some years ago I received a phone call from a man speaking English with an interesting accent. Calling on behalf of his father-in-law, who had just arrived from China, he wanted me to go to the West Coast to see him. Because the mission agency I served had great interest in China, I was glad to oblige. On the airplane I was quite excited in thinking I would at last get a firsthand answer to a question that had puzzled me for years: How did Christianity in Communist China grow from 500,000 believers in 1949 (when the missionaries were expelled) to over 50,000,000 believers in the early 1980's. I had heard different explanations—supernatural healings, the underground church, Christian programs on shortwave radio—but I was still curious.

As I sipped a cup of tea with Mr. Lee, I asked my question through his daughter, who translated and interpreted. He explained that he had just been released from four years in prison because of his faith. That was only one of several such imprisonments he had endured because he persisted in preaching the gospel. His answer to my question was simply, "Suffering." He explained that Christians in China have been persecuted greatly but have borne it patiently and lovingly. As their countrymen have observed this, responding rightly to rejection did far more than miracles or missionaries could ever do.

Blessed are the Blessers

Jesus' next commanded response to rejection is: "Bless those who curse you" (Luke 6:28a). Again, Jesus takes for granted that his followers would be cursed for their beliefs. He had just said, "Woe to you when all men speak well of you, for that is how their fathers treated the false prophets" (v.26). Do you want everybody to speak nicely of you? So did the false prophets, but that is hardly the group with which you want to be identified. What should be our response when we are cursed? Bless them. The word *bless* in Greek is *eulogia*. Although today "eulogize" means to say nice things about people after they have died, Jesus was not restricting his directive to that kind of commendation. "Eulogy" is from two Greek words; *eu* meaning "good" and *logos* meaning "word"—good word. So we are to speak good words to our cursers. We are not to curse them back, but neither are we to use flattery, lies, or sarcasm.

Again, we must try to see others from God's point of view. God can find something good about the person who is cursing you, and he loves that person as much as he loves you. To see through God's eyes, we must escape our own subjectivity; we must get out of ourselves and look at everyone objectively. Focus on the inner needs that would cause a person to curse you. Perhaps specific images are popping into your mind as you think about this—co-workers, neighbors, relatives, long-term enemies, authority figures—people who at one time have cursed you. Can you sincerely bless them by speaking positively about and to them? Your Lord can and wants you to also.

But isn't that dishonest? Not at all. Is it more honorable to curse back for the sake of honesty? A sick trend of our age suggests that we should let it all hang out, expose our negative feelings for the therapeutic value. Such a response, even if it were

> When we look at others through God's eyes, it is possible to respond in a loving way even to our enemies.

healthy for you (which I doubt), may do immeasurable damage to the person with whom you are being honest. It's a question of motive. Are you trying to restore your enemy or recover your wounded pride? Venting your hostile emotions fails to get at the real heart issues. Maybe your inner feelings are inappropriate because they are wrapped inside a layer of shortsighted subjectivity. True mental and emotional health requires us to become more objective in our outlook.

This is not to suggest that we become emotionless, but that our feelings must not be allowed to destroy our objectivity. We should allow thoughts and emotions to work together and lead us in the appropriate direction. This was why Jesus, and Stephen after him, could sincerely pray for forgiveness to be extended to his assassins. A purely emotional response, retaliation or retreat, reveals that we are self-absorbed. Remember, Jesus said that disciples who are persecuted *for his sake* are blessed. If we can realize that we are being cursed for that reason, we are well on the way toward objectivity and the right response: compassion.

But is such impartiality really possible? It was for David. On probably the saddest day of his life, David was able to respond with grace to a man cursing him and showering him with stones and dirt. David was fleeing his palace and Jerusalem, the City of David, because his rebellious son Absalom had arranged a conspiracy so that he could take his father's kingdom. As David fled, Shimei, a man of Saul's clan, came out cursing and taunting David with insults. Abishai, the same man who had encouraged David to kill Saul, volunteered to cut off Shimei's head.

David, however, said that perhaps God had a message for him through Shimei's cursing. (See 2 Samuel 16:5-13; 19:16-23.) That is true objectivity. We should note that there will always be an Abishai encouraging us to fight for our rights and, unknowingly, to surrender our honor. An outstanding and very entertaining book that delves deeply into this subject is Gene Edwards' *A Tale of Three Kings.*[4]

Tough Praying

The fourth admonition in this passage is to "pray for those who mistreat you" (Luke 6:28b). Again, Jesus assumes that his followers will be mistreated. Paul said that "everyone who wants to live a godly life in Christ Jesus will be persecuted" (2 Tim. 3:12). This is not a license to develop a martyr complex or to become a spiritual masochist as a step toward piety.

> The goal of Christ-likeness will never be achieved apart from learning how to respond to mistreatment.

It is just a simple statement. If you live a righteous life, people are going to mistreat you. We are to welcome such trials, not as a badge of saintliness, but as an opportunity for character development. The goal of Christ-likeness will never be achieved apart from learning how to respond to mistreatment.

What are we supposed to do to those who mistreat us? Pray for them, for they have a problem! As in the other three instructions, our focus ought to be on the welfare of the other person, not on his rejection of us. Do not respond in like manner to the rejection, the enmity, the hatred, the cursing, or the mistreatment. Instead, treat the other person as someone in need. See him from God's point of view and love the person whom the Lord loves. This cuts right across the grain of our natural instincts, which tell us to be defensive, protective, retaliatory. But Jesus is saying that is not what kingdom living is all about.

If you have a difficult time praying, try praying for someone who is mistreating you and all your other praying will seem easy. It is so very hard to pray for a person who despises you, abuses you, and is working toward your downfall. But do it anyway. Do it out of obedience to the Lord and out of compassion for your abuser. Many biblical scholars are convinced that the pricks of conscience that Paul had kicked against prior to his conversion (see Acts 26:14) came from the godly way Stephen responded to his martyrdom, which Paul had witnessed and apparently approved of. Imagine the great loss to the Christian cause had Stephen responded otherwise! In the midst of his severe mistreatment, Stephen prayed for those hurling the stones at him. Who knows what tremendous potential for the cause of Christ there might be in the very person who is mistreating you!

An interesting progression is found in these four responses to rejection: As your abuser becomes more identifiable, the command becomes more demanding and specific. Your "enemies" are people who just do not like you. You may or may not know who they are, but your response should be love. That does mean taking action, but the activity is not specified. The next abusers are more identifiable: "those who hate you." You are more likely to know who such a person is, and you must "do good" to him or her. Even more obvious to you is someone who "curses you." In return, bless the curser. Most recognizable are "those who mistreat you." Pray for them. As the abuser becomes more identifiable, it is incumbent upon you to become more active in that person's behalf. The greater the abuse, the greater the need; the greater the need, the more compassion is required.

Modified Pacifism?

Luke 6:29-30 gives several examples of a compassionate, non-retaliatory response to aggression:

> *If someone strikes you on one cheek, turn to him the other also. If someone takes your cloak, do not stop him from taking your tunic. Give to everyone who asks you, and if anyone takes what belongs to you, do not demand it back.*

Does this sound as if the Lord is setting up his people for some major abuse by demanding a lifestyle that may antagonize others, and then possibly adding injury to insult by not allowing us to defend ourselves? Volunteers for this kind of life probably won't have to stand long in line waiting for a ticket. But did Jesus truly mean it that way? Is there no moderation of this principle? Fortunately there is. It is not my desire to take any of the grit out of the gospel, especially since I have already suggested that the power of the gospel is seen most clearly in its radical contrast to the ways of the world. But I believe a few modifications of this pacifist principle are essential and legitimate.

First, we must note that Jesus gave this turn-the-other-cheek ethic with the assumption that the abuse is specifically related to our stand as Christian disciples. You are blessed "...when men hate you, when they exclude you and insult you and reject your name as evil, *because of the Son of Man"* (Luke 6:22, emphasis added). The apostles kept that qualifier in the formula also: "If you are insulted *because of the name of Christ*, you are blessed, for the Spirit of glory and of God rests on you" (1 Peter 4:14, emphasis added).

The point may be debatable, but criminal violence directed upon us that is not because of our Christian stand may not demand such a passive response. For example, to take an extreme, should a Christian father passively watch as a thief plunders his house, rapes his wife, and carries away his children? Does God require us to stand by idly, saying, "God bless you, brother. Please read this gospel tract?" No! We are expected to take care of our family. But if violence and ensuing suffering directed at us are overtly due to our Christian life, we must endure it. If we are the random victims of criminal activity, I believe it would be ungodly to tolerate the attack. Since proper self-protection is demanded of a faithful steward, it is part of a godly ministry. Even then, restraining, rather than harming the opponent is preferable.

A second qualifier is that the pacifist approach applies to need, not greed, and to constituted authority, not random bullying. Surrendering property to one in need is very different from allowing someone to feed his greed at your expense. Food and clothing are needs; a laptop computer or car is not.

The text does not tell us to give specifically what people ask for. What they ask for may not be what they need. A more godly response is to give to their real need. God does not always give us what we request, which is a good thing because we do not know what is best for us. He always gives us what we need. To respond to another person's true need may take more time and involvement than meeting their wants, but that is the kingdom way. Furthermore, it's one thing for legitimate authorities to seize my property (rightly or wrongly); it may be quite another thing to comply with organized crime. The examples Jesus used imply this. Again, the point is debatable, but re-read Luke 6:27-36 with these thoughts in mind. Also read Luke 3:7-14 and decide for yourself if this is not the intent of the teaching of both Jesus and John the Baptist.

Paul's life shows the latter distinction. He was passive to the Jewish authorities when he appeared before the Sanhedrin, but he would not give in to an illegal conspiracy of more than forty Jews who had plotted to kill him (Acts 23:12ff). When constituted authority, which has been established by God (Romans13:1) causes us to suffer, we must bear it, but we need not acquiesce to random bullying that is independent of our Christian commitment.

Nevertheless, the Christian response to all violence must be restraint, not retaliation or revenge. This is a matter of attitude and intent. Restraint opposes the evil being done while still hoping for a positive outcome for the enemy. Retaliation's intent is to hurt the offender; revenge is taken for the purpose of salving our own wounded spirit by getting even.

Do not be vengeful or try to retaliate against an aggressor. And do not be worried about your right to dignity and protection, for God will take care of you. "If someone takes your cloak, do not stop him from taking your tunic." In other words, do not be overly protective of your possessions. Because God can take care of your material needs, "Give to everyone who asks you, and if anyone takes what belongs to you, do not demand it back." Perhaps of all the commands of Christianity this is the toughest and most demanding.

Leon Morris provides a commentary on this passage:

> *If Christians took this one absolutely literally, there would be a class of saintly paupers owning nothing and another of prosperous idlers and thieves. It is not this that Jesus is seeking, but it is readiness among his followers to give and give and give. The Christian should never refrain from giving out of a love for his possessions. Love must be ready to be deprived of everything if need be. Of course, in a given case, it may not be the way of love to give. But it is love that must decide whether we give or withhold, not a regard for our possessions.[5]*

This view is exactly right for Christians who are responding to human need out of their individual resources. Who has not walked the streets of a busy city like New York or Chicago without brushing past outstretched begging hands? Overseas it is even worse, and we are warned by our tour guides, "Do not give them anything." But how is the gospel to be seen in that kind of callous nonresponse?

There are no easy answers to this complex issue, but we will be far better prepared to obey Jesus literally if we can draw form the courage, compassion, and resources of a closely knit body of disciples. Although sometimes, like Peter, we may need to say, "Silver or gold I do not have," we, too, should be willing to add, "but what I have I give you" (Acts 3:6). The church that seeks as a body to "give to everyone who asks" will not be short on ministry or fail to get recognition as a beacon of God's kingdom.

Always Golden

Then Jesus gave us an always dependable guideline: "Do to others as you would have them do to you" (Luke 6:31). It is interesting that it was in the context of responding to our enemies that Jesus taught this Golden Rule. Since we always want to be loved, blessed, treated well, and prayed for, we must treat other people that way, especially our enemies.

The rest of this passage explains that if we respond generously only to our loved ones or in expectation of a return, without going beyond to this godly principle, we are not better than sinners. They do such things: They love their friends and lend to people because they expect to get back exactly what they lend. We dare not feel good about ourselves if we are only doing what a sinner would do. If, however, our giving goes beyond self-interest, we are living according to the kingdom quality of compassion.

The key to modeling this radical lifestyle effectively is not for a few individuals to respond obediently, for it is easy for skeptics to explain away isolated extremism. But when a whole body of people, who in every other way are "sane," are seen to be compassionate, others will be encouraged to obey Jesus literally also. This principle has potential to shake up the community, the state, the nation, and the world. Whenever the kingdom of God is acting in power, the Spirit of God is renewing the church, and evangelism is going forward dynamically, it is because we Christians are taking these teachings very seriously. Jesus blesses obedience, not excuses.

Discipleship Principle #4: Responding to Rejection

Activating this discipleship principle may be a great challenge to your courage and inner strength, but unless the Lord's people learn to suffer rejection and respond to hostility as he did, we will never help others behold his kingdom. Only by developing compassion can we obey Discipleship Principle #4:

Discipleship Principle #4
In kingdom living, disciples of Jesus Christ respond to hostility and rejection by treating their enemies as well as they want to be treated themselves.

Chapter 5

EXAMINING MYSELF: INTEGRITY

Luke 6:37-49

Discipleship Principle #5
Rather than focusing on the failures and inadequacies of others, disciples of Christ periodically engage in healthy self-evaluation to assess their own spiritual status.

As the DC-10 headed toward Los Angeles, joy, excitement, an a twinge of smugness had my spirits soaring higher than the clouds. Hadn't I been personally recruited by an executive "headhunter" to be considered for the presidency of an international mission? Weren't my years of patience as a "number two" finally paying off? Wasn't this interview really a formality, as it was almost certain that I was the man for the job? Nevertheless, I was enjoying the courtship stage of what would undoubtedly be a great relationship. California, here I come!

The executive-search consultant and I spoke openly and freely over our stir-fry cuisine that evening. Bob's questions were penetrating, almost threatening, but I thought I handled them well. The next day we would meet with the board of directors of the mission for the official interview, and I expected to be offered the job soon afterward. Imagine—President, the CEO. I wanted to be where the buck stops, so I was ready.

Or so I thought. That night in the Sheraton was surely the most restless night of my life. Bob had unknowingly exposed a raw nerve in my psyche, and the twinge became more irritating and condemning throughout the night. One of his questions had something to do with how I handle conflict with other employees, especially those whom I do not particularly respect. Bob asked whether such people would make it in my organization. Could I welcome opposing viewpoints without considering the other person to be an opponent?

On the surface it seemed that I could give a favorable answer to that question, as I did during the discussion with Bob. But I knew that underneath lay another issue that might disqualify me from the top leadership position. During the night the Lord clarified and underscored that issue so emphatically that by morning I knew I was not ready for the job. I caught an early plane back to the East, licking my wounds, half-mad at God and very disappointed in myself. It was like appearing for dress inspection before the sergeant, only to find my belt missing.

What was that deeper issue? A critical and unforgiving spirit. Two Scriptures put the spotlight on that problem for me: "Bear with each other and forgive whatever grievances you may have against one another" (Col. 3:13a), and "Do not judge, and you will not be judged. Do not condemn, and you will not be condemned..." (Luke 6:37). As a manager, of course, my responsibilities included correcting and admonishing the workers, but it was now apparent to me that I had a tendency to write off anyone who did not think as I did, and then justify this by finding a spiritual

> Could I welcome opposing viewpoints without considering the other person to be an opponent?

inadequacy in that person. To determine whether I was just being overly self-critical, when I arrived home I told this story to a trusted friend and asked his perspective. Yes, he assured me, this did seem to be a pattern in my life; I tended to turn a person with an opposing view into an adversary. This was undermining my integrity as a Christian and my effectiveness as a manager. Since then, I have been learning to temper my judgmentalism, for I now realize how hypocritical it is to find fault with others while remaining blind to my own shortcomings.

Keeping Balance

Honest self-examination must balance and curb our impulse to focus on the inadequacies of others. On the other hand, while Christians are to be tolerant and forbearing with one another, we should not be indulgent or naïve. As will be shown in chapter 13, we are mutually accountable and have the responsibility to admonish and exhort one another about the principles of kingdom living. I am not advocating a say-nothing-and-look-the-other-way approach to Christian responsibility but the balance and sensible perspective emphasized in Luke 6:37-49.

Some people go to the opposite extreme by harshly judging themselves and becoming extremely introspective. Christians can become nearly paranoid with insecurity about their relation-ship with the Lord, viewing God as a strict disciplinarian who is easily angered and offended. After the slightest step out of line, they expect a spiritual spanking. These same Christians assume they never have the right to admonish another person because "Who am I? I'm not perfect either."

How, then, should we understand Jesus' teaching about not judging others? Anyone with an active brain forms opinions. We cannot get away from it. As moral creatures we constantly make assessments about conduct and behavior in the light of what we believe to be right. And as Christians our standards are very high, based upon no less than God's authoritative Word.

Yet we know, and the world also knows, and holds us accountable to, the familiar verse "Judge not." This seems like a real predicament. How can we retain our moral sensitivity and high standards without becoming judgmental outwardly or inwardly? Being silently judgmental may be more of a problem than overt, up-front criticism because it tears down relationships without giving other people an opportunity to vindicate themselves or seek improvement.

Church members have frequently said to me something like, "Pastor, are you aware of what [so-and-so] did [or said]? I know I'm being a bit judgmental, but..." Several questions would occur to me in those situations:

- Is this person gossiping or seeking help? (Thus *I* had to make a judgment!)
- Am I in danger here of sanctioning this judgmental attitude?
- How can I help this person see that he is asking me to be tolerant of his intolerance?
- Is this person really judging or merely being discerning?

Since this last distinction is legitimate, we will explore it in depth, but the claim to be discerning can too easily be used to excuse our sin of judging. We often call our sins by more acceptable names to exonerate our unbiblical behavior. The classic example is gossiping under the guise of sharing a prayer request. More subtly, we steal time from work to "serve the Lord"; view questionable films and literature to "stay current"; break relationship "for the sake of truth"; or indulge materialistic impulses to "earn peer respect."

There are dozens of other ways we sugar-coat our sins. Christians play not only mind-games, but also spirit-games. Eric Berne's *Games People Play* could well be adapted with a study of how we Christians mask our sins. A disciple who received one of the highest possible commendations was Nathanael, in whom Jesus saw "nothing false" (John 1:47; "no guile" in NKJB). If we are to grow in our discipleship, we must become like Nathanael in this area. The kingdom quality of *integrity* is essential in all spheres of our lives, but especially in our relationships with God's people.

The Folly of Judgmentalism

Certainly, judging others is sin, but given the humorous imagery of Luke 6:39, 41-42, Jesus obviously wanted his disciples to see that a judgmental attitude is also downright foolish. Several reasons are suggested in support of this idea.

All in the Family

Is it not foolish to judge others when we, too, will be judged (v.37)? Although neither our relationship with God nor our salvation is dependent upon our behavior or performance, Scripture consistently teaches that our fellowship with God is damaged by our sinning. Our heavenly Father will not overlook our mistreatment of his other children. When we judge them rather than forgive or be more patient, we assume a stance of superiority, which God detests. By doing so we put ourselves under God's judgment. If for none other than the selfish reason of avoiding being judged by God in this area, we ought to refrain from judging others.

Since judgmentalism does not jeopardize our salvation, in what sense will it earn for us the judgment of God? One commentator suggests that as we judge others we remove ourselves from the realm of God's abiding grace. A little-known principle of the life of the Spirit is: No grace to those who do not give grace; abundant grace to the gracious. This is not a matter of merits or awards; God is not "getting even" with those who do not extend grace. It is just that God refuses to reward those who reject his ways. Parents frequently and rightly use this principle in raising their children. A son who is continually nasty to his sister is mistreating his parents' daughter and thereby does not deserve privileges. If we keep in mind the family status we share with our fellow believers, we will understand God's attitude toward our judging his other children.

Two kinds of judgment are forbidden in verse 37. The first word, translated "judge," refers to making an assessment or coming to a conclusion about someone's conduct or motive. It is disallowed because our insight into another person is always incomplete, and therefore our judgment will always be based on partial evidence. "Condemn" is an intensified form of the same Greek word, but it carries the additional idea of imposing a sentence of guilt on the other person. This is wrong not only because of our incomplete knowledge, but because it is not our prerogative to usurp our Creator's judicial role.

Blind Guiding

Another reason judging others is foolish is suggested in verse 39. When we judge others, we are sure to embarrass ourselves. Why one blind person would attempt to lead another blind person is difficult to imagine, but it happens all the time in the Christian world. According to Jesus, the destination of the blind-leading-the-blind is "a pit." This pit is a place of destruction, a dead end that leads nowhere. As people who are surely blind to our own faults and even more blind to the true situation of others, we will inevitably lead ourselves and others off the track and into trouble if we persist in judging. This is both destructive and humiliating.

Each of us can probably cite stories of how hasty judgments have been proven wrong. A friend of mine, who holds to values similar to my own, found himself quite chagrined one time in church. It seems that every summer a well-known and very successful pastor from the Midwest takes an extended vacation in New England where my friend lives. Quite unassumingly he attends the same small rural church each summer and is asked to preach occasionally. Few of the parishioners know of this man's celebrity status, which is just fine with him. He sees himself only as a servant of God.

My friend's first exposure to this minister did not impress him favorably. The long white hair was a bit too much image-cutting, and the excessive jewelry—especially the gaudy bracelets—smacked of showmanship to my friend. Why would anyone, let alone a pastor, choose to wear so many flashy bracelets? One Sunday, when this man was being introduced to preach, my friend felt like walking out. He wondered why this flamboyant fellow was even being allowed to stand behind the pulpit and what he could possibly have to say on behalf of God.

The introduction continued, and the sights and gun barrel of my friend's judgment were turned on himself when he learned about the missionary zeal of this man of God and how the bracelets had been made for him by an African orphan he had "adopted," and he wore them as prayer reminders. Whatever message the man delivered that morning mattered little to my friend. He had already heard from God. In that worship service my friend's scorn turned to shame, which became repentance and then thanksgiving. For him the words, "Judge not" now wear many bracelets. A man's bracelets are his own business.

The Eye of the Hypocrite

A third folly in judging others is that while failing to see our own faults, we disclose them to others. Jesus used another humorous metaphor to convey this idea. Verses 41 and 42 picture a person with a plank in his eye trying to remove a speck of saw-dust from someone else's eye. The plank-eyes person is called a hypocrite by Jesus. That word comes from a Greek root that refers to playing a part on the stage with masks. A hypocrite is a super-critic who feigns virtues he does not possess but judges others for not measuring up to those very standards.

Lest we think that hypocrisy pertains only to the ungodly, let us remember that the man "after God's own heart," King David, provided one of the most glaring examples. His sins of adultery and murder were two huge planks in his eyes that blinded him to his own moral failure. The prophet Nathan told him the story about the rich man who, rather than slaughtering one of his many sheep or cattle to serve a meal to a guest, stole a precious little ewe lamb from a poor man. David's moral indignation was raised, and he was prepared to execute the rich man, until Nathan said, "You are the man!"—reminding the king of how grievously he had sinned (see 2 Samuel 12:1-10). Undoubtedly, the finger of hypocrisy has been pointed at all of us at one time or another, perhaps not as dramatically as in David's case, but the difference is only in degree. David responded properly by confessing and repenting, as should we.

Too often, unchurched people label churchgoers as hypocrites, and they are right. The world has only two kinds of people: hypocrites and forgiven hypocrites. The teaching of Jesus about judging should not discourage us from having high standards; rather, it should prompt us to see the failures of others as reminders to examine ourselves.

Having a plank in my eye obviously disqualifies me from extracting a speck from another person's eye. The ultimate irony is that after I have extracted my own plank, it is likely that the speck in the other's eye will no longer be visible to me. What I thought was his speck may have been my plank all along. This is like using a hand-held camera and assuming that clouds have covered the sun, when in reality my own thumb is over the lens. Move the thumb and the clouds are gone; remove my own plank and the other person's speck will likely be gone as well.

A teacher who upgraded from using a wall-mounted marker board in the classroom decided to go high tech and use PowerPoint to project onto the wall. In the midst of his lesson, wanting to change a word, he picked up the eraser and began wiping the wall. When the students laughed, he sensed his foolish act, went to the computer, and made the change there. The word was no longer on the wall! How often we are critical of the wall when in reality *we* are projecting the very thing that needs to be changed.

Two Warnings

Although the imagery changes, the next three verses (Luke 6:43-45) suggest two more reasons why judging others is foolish. For one thing, judging others is a sure way of revealing the wickedness of our own hearts. Just as the fruit of a tree reveals the tree's species, so does the fruit of our lives tell what kind of people we are. Our observers know that judging is wrong (even if they practice it themselves), and they know when they see someone being judgmental. Jesus said that the mouth speaks out of the overflow of the heart. If people hear us say damaging, hurtful things about others, they can be quite sure that those comments are not coming from a righteous and loving heart.

Teacher Bill Gothard suggests "Six Basic Indicators That Expose a Judgmental Spirit":

1. If his failure improves the opinion I have of myself, I am judging.
2. If his failure decreases my concern for the faults I know I have, I am judging.
3. If his failure gives me a desire to see that he is punished, I am judging.
4. If I am eager to tell others about his failure, I am judging.
5. If his failure prompts me to review his past failures, I am judging.
6. If his failure causes me to feel that I cannot forgive him, I am judging.[6]

The common factor in all these warnings is motive. In chapter 4 we examined the biblical way to respond to enemies. Even when someone is our enemy, God expects us to yearn for the best for that person. I suspect that usually the people we judge are not enemies but other Christians. We hold them to a higher standard than the world does, of course, but do we honestly yearn for the best for them?

A final reason why it is sheer folly to judge others is that evil always exposes itself anyhow. Bad fruit is easy to detect, so the bad tree will soon be known. Nevertheless, God would rather have us try to nurture it back to health than cut it down. If we start swinging an axe, we may discover that the axe is double-bladed, and the recoil may be very painful.

No Surprises!

How Jesus' teaching about judging relates to the kingdom quality of integrity may not be self-evident, so perhaps a few words about that will be helpful. The root meaning of the word *integrity* is oneness. The words *integer* (one whole number) and *integrate* (bringing into oneness) are other derivatives.

Oneness implies wholeness, all-togetherness. Because a person with integrity has organized a code of behavior around a central core of values, he or she is always the same person in every situation. There is no insincerity, duplicity, or hypocrisy in such a person. Someone has said that the true test of character is what a man does when he is alone. A man of integrity offers no surprises; he is thoroughly predictable, once we know his convictions.

> A man of integrity offers no surprises; he is thoroughly predictable, once we know his convictions.

God's kingdom is the realm of integrity, and his people are to be signs of that kingdom. The church is the practice field for the real game out in the world; the church is to be the place where we Christians learn from our mistakes, receive coaching, and prepare for the competition, where we are always the visiting team. Since the home-field advantage belongs to the world, acting with integrity toward our team members is an essential part of our game plan.

A man or woman of integrity has achieved a state of internal unity, the ability to "will one thing," which is how Bonhoeffer described purity of heart. That one thing is the kingdom of God, where all its subjects strive for peace, harmony, and goodwill. One of the phrases describing true love is that it "keeps no record of wrongs" (1 Cor. 13:5). I knew one misguided Christian who kept a "gotcha" booklet on other believers who had either offended him or were guilty of some other sin. When I asked him why he kept it, he replied, "Just in case." "Just in case of what?" I asked incredulously. "Just so these people get what's coming to them if it's ever necessary. I have the proof!" Needless to say, this gentleman was struggling in his Christian growth. When Christians relish exposing other Christians, the body of Christ suffers terribly. Integrity demands that we acknowledge our own flaws as sincerely as we encourage others.

To Judge or Not to Judge

Up to this point we have been reaffirming and supporting what the Bible makes very obvious: judging others is sin. Few commands of Jesus are stated so simply and so clearly. There is not much chance of misunderstanding the statement "Judge not." But did you notice that in the same context and on the same occasion, Jesus also spoke about trees being known by their fruit? In Matthew's parallel account of this teaching, Jesus seemed to undermine the entire business of not judging by using three pejorative terms. He warned his followers, "Do not give dogs what is sacred; do not throw your pearls to pigs" (Matt. 7:6a), and "Watch out for false prophets..." (v.15). Obviously, in order to detect dogs, pigs, and false prophets some kind of judgment must be made. So we are back to judging. Or are we?

Three very important facts solve this dilemma. The first relates to the audience being addressed, the second considers historical background, and the third concerns the Greek words that were used.

Singular or Plural?

Often in the Bible it is not immediately apparent to whom a particular message was being given. The English pronoun "you" is both singular and plural, which can cause considerable confusion. For example, when Jesus said to Peter, "I will give you the keys of the kingdom of heaven" (Matt. 16:19), did the "you" refer to Peter himself (singular), or to all the disciples and/or all Christians (plural)? The Greek language uses different words for singular and plural pronouns, so it is clear that Jesus meant this for Peter alone. In English the context usually helps us know whom the writer meant, but not always.

Generally we observe in Scripture that wherever judging is allowed, that judgment is to be made by a group or someone representing the group, not by an individual. Although in the case of the command to "judge not," Jesus was addressing a group and the plural form was used, when he illustrated his point, he used examples of individuals (the blind guide and the man with the plank in his eye). The context therefore suggests that this type of judging is forbidden for an individual. Under certain circumstances, judgment by a group is not only permissible – it is expected. For example, Paul rebuked the church for not judging a sinful man (1 Cor. 6:1-6).

Law in the Right Hands

The second determinant of whether judging is allowed requires that we understand some historical and cultural background. You have probably heard people say that they much prefer the God of the New Testament to the God of the Old. The

God of the Old Testament is thought to be vengeful and harsh, whereas the New Testament God is seen to be merciful and loving. Did God change? Did he mellow with old age? Of course, such thoughts are absurd and unworthy of God. Jesus' words in another passage are particularly helpful here: "You have heard that it was said 'Eye for eye, and tooth for tooth.' But I tell you, do not resist an evil person. If someone strikes you on the right cheek, turn to him the other also" (Matt. 5:38-39).

> The God of the Old Testament is thought to be vengeful and harsh, whereas the New Testament God is seem to be merciful and loving. Did God change?

Was Jesus changing the eye-for-eye law given in Exodus 21:24? It appears that way, but not so. The Old Testament laws were given for the people to obey, but the penalties were given for the *leaders* to enforce. That is why the first leaders of the Israelites were called "judges." The eye-for-eye law was never meant for people to use vengefully or to take the law into their own hands, which had been happening when Jesus gave this correction. It was meant as a guideline for the judges.

Word Ambiguity

An examination of some of the Greek words used for the idea of judging is also useful. By now you have no doubt realized that the word *judge* is ambiguous, so it should not be surprising that there are several Greek words used to express slightly different aspects of judging. Without becoming too technical, it is helpful to note five different ways the New Testament refers to judging. One word is about *testing*, in the sense of proving the worthiness of a thing or person. It is chiefly used to encourage us to examine ourselves (1 Cor. 11:28), to test the spirits (1 John 4:1), or to prove all things (1 Thess. 5:21).

The other four Greek words are all derived from a word that means "to judge." One has to do with *investigating* facts to verify truth. This word is used about the people of Berea, who "examined the Scriptures" to determine whether Paul's message was true (Acts 17:11). The same word is used about Pilate's examination of Jesus (Luke 23:14). Another word refers to *discerning* or distinguishing between things or people. The messages of prophets, for example, are to be weighed carefully (1 Cor. 14:29), presumably to differentiate between the true and the false. These three types of "judging" are valid activities and not forbidden. In fact, testing, investigating, and discerning are legitimate and important endeavors for all who honor truth and righteousness, for rightly motivated discernment comes from God. Oswald Chambers said, "God never gives us discernment in order that we may criticize, but that we may intercede."

The other two words, the ones used in our text, are translated "judge" and "condemn." Both are forbidden. The first means to separate, or *distinguish and then make a preferential choice*. This sounds harmless enough, except that when it comes to making moral judgments, we are all eminently unqualified, for one simple reason – moral actions come from a person's soul, or as Jesus said, "out of the overflow of his heart" (Luke 6:45). None of us is able to read another person's soul, so our judgments must be based entirely on external behavior, which is not fair. Morals boil down to motives, and none of us can know the motives of another person. (A man's bracelets are his own business.)

The fifth word is the most extreme: *condemn*. The force here is on meting out a damning sentence. The offending party is tried, found guilty, and condemned. There may or may not be justice, but there is closure. The same reason that disqualifies all humans from "judging" certainly excludes us from "condemning." Even our sinless Lord, who alone was qualified to condemn, refused to do so. Given the chance to show his high standards and at the same time earn favor with the Jewish leaders by affirming what the law provided—the stoning of a woman caught in adultery—Jesus refused to condemn: "neither do I condemn you," he told her after the eager stone-hurlers had already departed in shame. Hoping to make sport of both the woman and Jesus, they were instead faced with their guilt and lack of credentials for judging when Jesus said, "If any one of you is without sin, let him be the first to throw a stone at her." (See John 8:1-11.)

This story precisely makes the point that the degree of our eagerness to expose and condemn another's wrongdoing matches the degree of our being unqualified to do so. Therefore, those who are most inclined to judge prove thereby that they should not, and those who are qualified to judge are usually the ones who refrain.

Rather than trying to remember the nuances of all these words, we might be best served by distinguishing between "discerning" and "judging." Bill Gothard contrasts them this way:[7]

Discerning

Thoroughly examines one's self before evaluating the actions of others
Checks the accuracy of all facts and related factors before reaching a conclusion
Deals as privately and humbly as possible to restore one who has stumbled

Judging

Condemns others for their visible problems, but does not see the underlying root attitude, which he also has
Forms opinions on hearsay and first impressions, then looks for evidence to confirm
Publicly exposes those he condemns

The Pygmalion Principle

The positive role that we play in a person's life by not being judgmental is a very powerful motivator. By refusing to look for the bad in a person, we necessarily choose to expect the best. Barnabas exemplified this in his reclaiming of John Mark from the rubbish heap of failure. During Paul's first missionary journey, John Mark abandoned Paul and his companions at Pamphylia (Acts 13:13). Later, when Barnabas wanted to give Mark a second chance, Paul refused, resulting in a separation between them. Barnabas took John Mark with him on a mission to Cyprus (Acts 15:39), where apparently Mark once again got on the road to a successful ministry. Even Paul acknowledged this later; in writing to Timothy he said, "Get Mark and bring him with you, because he is helpful to me in my ministry" (2 Timothy 4:11).

Barnabas, the encourager, used what today we call the Pygmalion principle. In George Bernard Shaw's play *Pygmalion*, later the theme for *My Fair Lady*, Professor Henry Higgins transforms a poor, crude Cockney flower girl into a lovely, sophisticated woman of good standing in London society. Pastor Don Bubna calls this the ministry of "Building People" in his book by that name. My friend Dick Walther, in a monthly leadership letter wrote, "Our attitude toward others and our related treatment of others has the power to transform. Our expectations bring about change in behavior." Speaking to managers, he gives eight ways for applying the Pygmalion principle.[8]

1. Be persuaded that everyone can do better and that most use only a fraction of their potential.
2. Demonstrate confidence in your staff.
3. Maintain dialogue, open communication, feedback.
4. Give your staff recognition.
5. Set high, yet achievable, standards.
6. Outlaw "put-downs" even if meant in jest.

7. Introduce new people as being special and assign a mentor or trainer who has motivating skills.
8. Control and correct prejudices which warp our perception of potential: culture, appearance, male/female, age.

Discipleship Principle #5: Examining Myself

We may not all be managers in the business world, but the principle of building up people rather than tearing them down by judging is certainly a Christ-like virtue. It also reflects the kingdom quality of personal integrity. The easiest way to refrain from destructive criticism is to heed Paul's counsel to those about to receive the Lord's Supper: "A man ought to examine himself before he eats of the bread and drinks of the cup...But if we judged ourselves, we would not come under judgment" (1 Corinthians 11:28, 31). To say it another way, we are to implement Discipleship Principle #5:

Discipleship Principle #5
Rather than focusing on the failures and inadequacies of others, disciples of Christ periodically engage in healthy self-evaluation to assess their own spiritual status.

PART TWO:

Learning Kingdom Ministry

Chapter 6

ACCEPTING HIS LORDSHIP: SELFLESSNESS

Luke 9:18-27

Discipleship Principle #6
Because disciples accept the Lordship of Christ, they value the cause of the kingdom far above their own happiness, convenience, comfort, and even their own existence.

The most basic lesson of discipleship was not the first one Jesus could teach. There were too many prejudices and preconceptions blocking the way, so he had to begin with some theological excavation.

When a contractor sets out to build a house, he must first clear away the brush, the topsoil, and rocky subsoil to reach a firm footing for his foundation. We call this process excavation. In human terms, sin, disbelief, and naturalism smother the soul, making it inhospitable to a solid theology. Jesus may have spent more than a year preparing the souls of his followers for the foundation of his kingdom, so it was not until the incident recorded in Luke 9:18-27 (parallels in Matthew 16:13-20 and Mark 8:27-38) that Jesus faced them squarely with the big issue: his identity.

All other issues and lessons become irrelevant if the identity of Jesus Christ is not comprehended. If he is not the king, there is no kingdom. If there is no kingdom, the human species is on its own forever—a bleak prospect indeed. But, like the first-century disciples, we may not be immediately ready to be faced with Jesus' big question: "Who do you say I am?" We need to know who we are (and who we are not) before we can grapple with the claims of Christ.

> If he is not the king, there is no kingdom. If there is no kingdom, the human species is on its own forever.

Cogito Ergo Sum!

The issue of our own identity is not a new one. Man has been looking for a sense of meaning, purpose, and value for centuries. Modern Western philosophy started with the question: "Who am I?" When Descartes came to the conclusion that at least he existed, he was attempting to solve his identity crisis through reasoning. His enlightened "I think, therefore I am" ushered in the age of rationalism. Although the human mind is not the highest form of intelligence that exists, Descartes's optimism is far more appealing than the kind of modern irrationalism expressed in a dour and sarcastic perversion of his words: "I drink, therefore I am." For many people, unfortunately, the meaning of their lives is totally wrapped up in how they can sate their sensual appetites.

That was surely the message Satan delivered to Eve. He tempted her to challenge God's authority through a sensory experience by which she hoped to achieve an identity beyond her known limitations. No different in essence from the hippies of the 1960s who took LSD for a transcendental peak experience. Andrew Weil calls it "achieving an altered state of consciousness."[9] How prone we are to trying to escape our sense of insignificance by sating our senses and dulling our minds. Why? Because the mind quickly reveals how finite and unimportant we are. In fact, the more we learn, the less significant we seem to be.

Who Am I?

I am a speck, just one tiny organism in what used to be considered a big planet but is now known also to be just a little speck in the universe. We know that if our solar system (the nine planets that circle the sun) were shrunk down to the size of a tennis ball, our galaxy would be the size of North America. And the Milky Way is just one of millions of galaxies that exist. So my mind tells me that I'm just one puny organism occupying one brief moment of time. Am I any more important than the leaves that fall off the tress in the autumn? Is my fate the same as theirs – just to become part of the soil? Something within me cries out, "NO, it can't be!" Is this only wishful thinking based on my desire for self-preservation? Or is there greater significance to the fact that within me are some extremely deep longings, aspirations, and abilities not seen anywhere else in nature?

Just the ability to reflect on such a question sets human beings apart from the rest of creation. We are told that worship behavior has been found in people of all cultures and in every era of recorded history. But is there a reason for my existence—and for yours? Why does this hide-and-seek God leave us with so many questions that can only be answered by faith? The origin of the universe? The meaning of life? The destiny of mankind?

We all have our own identity crisis. Jesus knew this as he looked into the lives of his disciples. He had with him men who were competitive, wanting to be the best, striving to get to the top. He had others who were insurrectionists, rebels at heart, eager to fight for lofty ideals. Others were materialistic and had pursued a life of financial gain and comfort. All of them were expressing in different ways this great drive toward finding meaning and personal identity in life.

Today we can go to any adult education center and take courses in self-authentication and ego-assertiveness to help us find or shape our identity. That's just the more adult way of doing what the young people did when they dropped out to hitchhike across the country, trying to "find themselves." It's all the same striving. Today, we are told that to really be someone you must assert yourself. You must climb to the top. Authenticate your existence. Be all that you can be. Go for it.

Being Incorporated

Way back in the Garden of Eden the first question God asked Adam was, "Where are you?" Adam's response was, "I heard you in the garden, and I was afraid because I was naked; so I hid" (Genesis 3:9, 10). He was not just physically naked; he was suddenly transparent, totally exposed as a sinner. Adam and Eve hid so well that they could not even find themselves. And that has been our problem all these years. We try to hide from the Source of life. And without him we cannot find ourselves.

Jesus gave us a clue to this whole problem. It is also part of the answer to another question: "What is a disciple?" This answer is found in Luke 9: we will truly find ourselves only when we lose ourselves and are found in Christ. Jesus was not talking here about losing our identity, our personality, our individuality, or our personhood. Underline the word *self* in verse 23, and you will understand what he meant. It is self-centeredness, self-absorption, and selfish interests that need to be denied. If not, you will lose your life; that is, your future is dead-ended. Why? Because apart from Christ, you have no future beyond your death. And apart from Christ, life does not make sense. As one dropout said, "Life is a joke and I'm the punch line."

Paul calls this experience being "in Christ," and that phrase has great meaning. It is the idea of kingdom incorporation. In Romans 5 Paul describes how all people are incorporated either "in Adam" or "in Christ." Adam, Inc. is bankrupt; it has no future. But Christ, Inc. is a blue-chip corporation all the way. It is not just a corporation. It is the eternal kingdom of God. Wise people are eager to invest their lives in Christ, Inc. They recognize the truth in these words of Jesus: "What good is it for a man to gain the whole world, and yet lose or forfeit his very self?" (Luke 9:25 NIV).

What does being incorporated "in Christ" involve? According to Luke 9, the terms of incorporation require three things: knowing who Jesus is (vv. 18-20), understanding the implications of discipleship (vv. 21-22), and following him by fully identifying with him (vv. 23-27).

Who is Jesus

First, let's consider the idea of knowing who Jesus is, acknowledging his identity. His first question to the disciples was not too threatening: "Who do the crowds say I am?" (v. 18). Jesus already knew the answer and he surely was not obsessed with crowd approval. He asked it to uncover and correct certain false notions about himself before revealing his true identity.

Earlier in the same chapter, Luke 9:7-9, we see that Herod was also concerned about the identity of Jesus. He had been hearing about the unusual teachings and miraculous activity of the Nazarene, and he was perplexed. He had beheaded John the Baptist, so Jesus could not be he. John was "a voice" (Luke 3:4), preparing the way for the Messiah, so Herod was right: Jesus was not John. Jesus is not merely a voice crying in the wilderness. He is not merely God's spokesman.

Knowing the Baptist was dead, others said that perhaps Jesus was Elijah. This was a teaching, which all the Jews knew, that Elijah would come back to earth. According to the Old Testament, Elijah did not die. He was transported into glory in a chariot of fire. The Jews believed (some still do) that just prior to the coming of Messiah, Elijah would reappear as a conscience, a prophetic voice to Israel. Jesus had many things in common with Elijah, but he was not merely a heroic figure like Elijah or any other prophet.

Those possibilities considered, Jesus then asked Peter, "But what about you? Who do you say I am?" Peter's affirmation, and it took a lot of courage for him to say this, was: "The Christ of God," meaning, the Messiah. This was not an emotional outburst by a religious fanatic having a "peak experience." It was said by an earthy, robust man who was walking with Jesus and trying to figure him out. This man had seen Jesus in a variety of situations. And he came to the conviction that Jesus was the promised Messiah, the Christ—"the Son of the living God" (Matthew 16:16).

In Matthew's account, Jesus replied, "Blessed are you, Simon son of Jonah, for this was not revealed to you by man, but by my Father in heaven" (Matthew 16:17). Special revelation enabled Peter to come to this understanding, the foundational truth of all Christianity and the key to the kingdom of God.

For us, twenty centuries after the events, making that declaration is easier than it was for people in the first century. This is why, after Peter declared Jesus to be the Christ, Jesus warned his followers not to tell anyone about him being the Messiah. The Jewish expectation of Messiah was far different from what Jesus presented. In fact, Paul called the idea of a crucified Messiah "a stumbling block to Jews and foolishness to Gentiles" (1 Corinthians 1:23). It would be offensive to Jews to think of the Messiah coming to earth to be killed by hanging on a cross, the expression of ultimate damnation as far as Jewish tradition was concerned. (See Deuteronomy 21:22-23) So, for most of them, it was quite difficult to believe that Jesus was more than a prophet.

Just to prove the truth of this amazing fact, God allowed Peter, James, and John to see the Son of Man coming into his kingdom glory, in the transfiguration experience (Luke 9:28-36). Lost for words in rapturous delight of seeing their glorified Master talking with Moses and Elijah, Peter proposed building three sanctuaries—one for Jesus, one for Moses, and one for

Elijah. A new trinity, presumably! Such heresy was soon interrupted by a bright cloud that enveloped them and a voice from the cloud saying, "This is my Son, whom I have chosen; listen to him." The voice was obviously the voice of God the Father, and this very dramatic authentication of Jesus' claims demands that we, too, accept Jesus as the unique Son of God.

Many cults and offshoots of Christianity talk about sonship in an entirely different way than the Bible puts it forth. Jesus had a one-of-a-kind sonship: *messiah sonship*. All who are born of God the Spirit are sons and daughters of God by adoption (see Ephesians 1:5 and Romans 8:23, 9:4). But Jesus was not adopted. The early church struggled with this mystery and affirmed its truth in the Nicene Creed. Here is what it says about Jesus:

> *[I believe] in one Lord Jesus Christ, the only begotten Son of God, Begotten of his Father before all worlds; God of God, Light of Light, very God of very God; Begotten, not made, Being of one substance with the Father; By whom all things were made; Who, for us men, and for our salvation, came down from heaven, And was incarnate by the Holy Ghost of the Virgin Mary, And was made man, And was crucified also for us under Pontius Pilate. He suffered and was buried; And the third day he rose again, according to the Scriptures; And ascended into heaven, And sitteth on the right hand of the Father, And he shall come again with glory to judge both the quick and the dead; Whose kingdom shall have no end.*

Notice in the beginning part of the creed the strong emphasis on this unique, mysterious, incomprehensible, total relationship between Jesus, the Son of God, and the Godhead: "God of God...very God of very God...Being of one substance with the Father." The Nicene Creed was written against a backdrop of a struggle over the dual nature of Jesus. Some said he was merely a man with a greater spark of deity than the rest of us. Others said he was God, appearing on earth in a phantom existence. And others tried to mix the two together in strange ways, mainly half and half, but even that is wrong.

The Bible affirms consistently that Jesus Christ is all God and all man. One plus one equals One! Yes, it's mysterious. But if you cannot accept the mystery, neither can you accept the existence of God. Those who refuse to allow for divine mystery in the universe make their finite mind to be the ultimate authority for what they believe. They become their own god.

To be incorporated "in Christ," we must know who he is. We must believe the voice from the cloud. That voice was not just teaching theology; God was revealing a relationship: "This is my Son...listen to him."

We can all cite the same creed. Millions do so every Sunday without being moved inwardly. Right theology does not guarantee spiritual conviction. To be part of Christ, Inc., we need to be convinced Sunday through Saturday that Jesus Christ is God. He is alive. He sits at the right hand of power today and is coming back as King. And there will be no rival authorities that can overcome him. We need to live with those truths and be committed to them daily. The Lordship of Jesus Christ is the foundation of discipleship.

What Did Being Messiah Entail?

As surprising as discovering Jesus' identity was for the disciples, learning what it meant for him was even more shocking. Imagine how they felt when Jesus said, "The Son of Man must suffer many things and be rejected by the elders, chief priests, and teachers of the law, and he must be killed and on the third day be raised to life" (Luke 9:22).

That must have seemed like a rather farfetched way of being Messiah. Didn't Jesus know these people had been waiting for a deliverer for hundreds of years? Did he really expect to be rejected by the Jewish authorities, the most religious people in society? Rejected and killed?

In chapter 4 we examined ways to respond to enemies, those who reject or abuse us. Surely the enemies of Jesus' disciples would be the Romans or Samaritans. But here he says he will be rejected by the elders, the chief priests, and scribes – his own people!

How did Jesus respond to this rejection? To be sure, he always confronted his enemies with truth, even the truth about themselves. This was done as an expression of love. He also prayed for them. He did not resist them. In all of this, Jesus was being faithful to his own identity. Because he knew who he was and why he had come, Jesus told his disciples that "the Son of Man did not come to be served, but to serve, and to give his life a ransom for many" (Matthew 20:28).

How Does One "Follow" Jesus?

Jesus' disciples probably knew all along he was not taking them on a glory road. If he was going to be persecuted, they would also suffer. And some of them would be killed. Yet they obeyed his words, "If anyone would come after me, he must deny himself and take up his cross daily and follow me" (Luke 9:23). These words were not given to be memorialized on walnut plaques in suburban homes. They are part of everyday kingdom living. If you want to follow Jesus, you must carry a cross on your back. As Bonhoeffer said, "The cross is laid on every Christian." We must fully identify with his plain as well as with his glory.

Paul told the church at Philippi to have the same attitude as that of Christ Jesus, who – being in the form of God – did not grasp after lofty heights of deity, but willingly came down and took upon himself the form of a man. He humbled himself and was obedient, even to death on the cross (Philippians 2:6-8).

113

Discipleship starts with this attitude. Are you seeking great things for yourself? Are you striving to get to the top? The only way we can be raised up with Jesus is to follow him through the suffering and rejection that culminated in his crucifixion.

My I.D.

It should now be obvious that knowing who Christ is and that his way leads to the cross – death to self – is a prerequisite to accepting his Lordship. This takes us back to the idea of incorporation in Christ. When we deny ourselves, take up the cross, and follow him, there is no question where we are going: Golgotha, the hill of crucifixion. Paul expressed this intimate sense of full identification with Christ when he told the wayward Galatians, "I have been crucified with Christ and I no longer live, but Christ lives in me. The life I live in the body, I live by faith in the Son of God, who loves me and gave himself for me" (Galatians 2: 20).

Paul was not referring to some metaphysical experience, a transplant of the spirit of Jesus into his body. He was speaking legally. The context is about the law and the believer's relationship to it. By appropriating Christ's death as my death, my penalty for sin, and by giving him authority over me, I become bound in a spiritual and legal covenant. No longer am I viewed as an independent agent. Whoever would relate to me, including God the Father, cannot relate to me as an individual, but must respond to the corporation. And that is how I can come to God through Jesus Christ in my incorporated capacity. God deals with those who are "in Christ" in terms of the corporate CEO: Jesus Christ.

In a day of self-indulgence, what does "denying myself" mean? Surely more is meant by selflessness than going off pizza for a week or making some other token act of sacrifice. Self-denial means ego transference, subordinating my sense of independence and me-ism to the cause of Christ. I thereby come to care more about what happens to the corporation than I care about just me personally. Getting a handle on this is difficult for those who have been brought up in the Western culture, where individualistic identity predominates. If you ask me who I am, I will tell you my name. But if you ask someone in an Oriental culture who he is, he will tell you his family's name or his tribe's name because he is part of them. The culture of Jesus and his disciples was more Oriental than Western, so perhaps they understood corporate identity more easily than we do. But denying self and living for another has never been easy. In commercial terms, it means being the total company man, sold out to the corporation. My corporation is the kingdom of God. Because I'm a kingdom man, my slogan is, "The kingdom first." Do I live it perfectly? Far from it. Does Christ? Yes, and I am glad to be in him.

Beyond the Burden

What does it mean to take up the cross? Often we define our cross as any burden that we are called on to bear—a problem in the family, a financial difficulty, a personality quirk, a physical handicap. Although these are real burdens, and Jesus cares about our inner struggles, that was not what he meant when he said, "Take up your cross." A cross is a device that will kill you, a symbol of total sacrifice. When we think of personal struggles as bearing a cross, we are focusing on legitimate human concerns: pain, inconvenience, and mental discomfort. But a cross is only a burden when you are carrying it, not when you are hung on it. The cross is where you find death to self. And when you find death to self, "for my sake," Jesus says, then, you have truly found life.

> People who live for and die for a king who cannot be seen will be held up for ridicule, persecution, and ostracism.

115

The true meaning of the cross reaches beyond the burden. A burdened person still puts his hope for fulfillment in plans, friends, possessions, and technology. A crucified man has none of these hopes for he has said his last "Good-bye" to all earthly attachments.

Henri Nouwen, in *Reaching Out*[10], speaks of this sense of going beyond the burden. Identifying with God in intimate incorporation, he suggests, goes beyond loneliness to solitude, beyond hostility to hospitality, and beyond illusion to prayer. In each case there is a sense of going beyond self.

Perhaps most difficult to accept is the death of our reputation, our respectability. Thus Jesus warned his followers about being ashamed of him, his way, and his words. In a naturalistic, rationalistic world, people who live for and die for a king who cannot be seen—a king who was crucified on a cross and whose power is seen in denial and death of self—will be held up for ridicule, persecution, and ostracism. It will be no different for the student than for the Master Teacher. As Bonhoeffer said, "When Christ calls a man, he bids him come and die."

The fundamental issue we are talking about is power: Who is in control? In a world of over six billion people, each competing for limited resources, for social recognition and personal rights, no wonder there is so much conflict, hostility, and warfare. Six billion gods are a lot to satisfy! As long as we continue to live for ourselves, fighting for our own comfort, convenience, and happiness, that is exactly the role we have chosen—to be our own god. Thus, we break the first commandment: "You shall have no other gods before me." The beauty of Christ's coming as God's Son and our Big Brother is that he enables us to enter the royal family without competing for divine status, but this is only accomplished by our submitting to his Lordship.

Discipleship Principle #6: Accepting His Lordship

We began this chapter by suggesting that this lesson in discipleship might be the most basic one. Surely it is. Until we get clearly in mind and heart that Jesus is Master, we cannot, will not, and should not follow him. Selflessness is a kingdom quality that leads us to say with Peter, "You are the Christ." It shows that we have opted for Discipleship Principle #6:

Discipleship Principle #6
Because disciples accept the Lordship of Christ, they value the cause of the kingdom far above their own happiness, convenience, comfort, and even their own existence.

Chapter 7

FOCUSING ON PRIORITIES: INTENSITY

Luke 9:57-62

Discipleship Principle #7
Discipleship demands singleness of purpose, which is demonstrated by a sense of extreme urgency for advancing God's kingdom.

In a layman's approach to personality theory, we rather simplistically refer to Type A and Type B personalities. Type A is usually a hard-driving, intense, perfectionist workaholic, while Type B is a more laid-back, relaxed, and contemplative individual. Surely there are more insightful and sophisticated personality classifications, but for our purpose here, Type A and Type B will do.

We should first understand that being a disciple is not dependent on having one personality or another. To reinforce this idea, notice the contrast between the kingdom quality in the previous chapter – selflessness—and the quality we will study here—intensity. We might be tempted to think that selflessness is a property of the Type B personality, whereas intensity belongs to Type A people. Perhaps a Type B would find it easier to grow in humility than would Type A, and a Type A might more naturally express intensity. However, the Master wants each of his disciples to mature in all fifteen kingdom qualities. You have now examined six of those qualities and certain ones probably seem more challenging, even more threatening, than others.

If you are reading this book with others in a small group, you will see other members responding quite differently than you do to each chapter. Not only has God created each of us as a unique individual, but our personalities develop with a great diversity that is shaped by both heredity and experience. Therefore, as we explore Luke 9:57-62 and consider intensity as a character quality of God's kingdom, do not hastily conclude that Jesus was extolling one personality type over another. The intensity that is important to Jesus refers to the fervor demonstrated by disciples who consider kingdom goals their top priority. That quality is unrelated to overall personality.

Furthermore, neither was Jesus recommending a particular lifestyle. In our day and society, many of us live at a hectic pace, moving from one activity to the next almost as if trying to rescue our furniture from a house fire. But Jesus was not pointing to a fast-paced lifestyle as evidence of spirituality. Many of the most effective disciples have seen the fruit of their ministry increase proportionately to the time given to prayer, meditation, and quiet conversation. They have learned that in the kingdom, as in business, working smarter, not harder and faster, yields the best results. The intensity that is so clearly the concern of Jesus has little to do with pace and everything to do with purpose and direction.

Righteous Intensity

Our Lord's earthly life was a study in righteous intensity. At age twelve, when he was left behind in Jerusalem by his earthly parents, Jesus was already ordering his priorities toward the work of God. When confronted by Mary and Joseph, who had anxiously looked for him for three days, he responded, "Did you not know that I must be about My Father's business?" (Luke 2:49 NKJB). This mission was later succinctly defined with these words: "The Son of Man came to seek and to save what was lost" (Luke 19:10). Luke also tells us that "As the time approached for him to be taken up to heaven, Jesus resolutely set out for Jerusalem" (Luke 9:51). In Isaiah's prophecy, this fierce determination is expressed picturesquely in our Redeemer's own words: "Because the Sovereign LORD helps me, I will not be disgraced. Therefore have I set my face like flint..." (Isaiah 50:7).

The most triumphant words uttered by our Savior were also the last before he died: "It is finished" (John 19:30). The intensity of Jesus in pursuing his God-given purpose on earth is evident throughout the Gospels, but it accurately reflects the intensity of God the Father, whose plan of redemption was set in motion immediately after the fall and will continue through history until its consummation with the return of Christ to set up his kingdom in full. The unswerving clarity of focus that is part of his own character is a kingdom quality Jesus looks for in his disciples. The top priority for a disciple should be the advancement of God's kingdom.

If Jesus were to come to you today and say, "Follow me," would you know what he meant? What would be your reply? The Gospels record the responses of some who heard those words, but we are left in the dark about others. Luke 9:57-62 tells about two men who volunteered to follow Jesus and another whom Jesus specifically called. This short passage contains three significant teachings of Jesus that refer to the intense dedication required of all those who want to be disciples. Our understanding of this particular text, however, depends on first examining several interesting events recorded in the preceding verses.

Law, Prophet, Son

We have already seen Peter's bold declaration of belief in Jesus as the Messiah, after which Jesus clearly spelled out the implications of submitting to his Lordship (see chapter 6). Next we find Peter, James, and John with Jesus on the Mount of Transfiguration, where the three apostles saw Jesus glorified and heard a heavenly voice telling them, "This is my Son, whom I have chosen; listen to him" (Luke 9:35). This statement was both an affirmation of Jesus' identity and a rebuke to the disciples, who were equating Jesus with Moses and Elijah. The voice nullified any thought that the law (Moses) and the prophets (Elijah) were equal in stature to the gospel (God's Son). "*This* is my Son...listen to *him*."

Here the disciples were learning a dramatic lesson about priorities, a lesson that three other would-be disciples would learn very soon. As important as the law and the prophets are in God's plan, they are superseded by Jesus Christ and his gospel. Therefore, Jesus cannot be just one part of a disciple's life. He must be everything — first and foremost.

Defining Allegiance

The Word of God goes on to record two related events in Luke 9 that refer to the dimension and quality of a disciple's faith. While Jesus and the three were on the mountain, the other nine apostles were down in the valley confronted by a difficult situation (Luke 9:37-43). A man had brought his demon-possessed son, his only child, to be healed. Not finding Jesus, he asked the nine disciples to drive out the demon. The man's great disappointment is revealed in his words, "...but they could not." Jesus was equally disappointed with the failure of his men — the parallel passage in Matthew has the disciples asking Jesus why they were not successful, and Jesus answering, "Because you have so little faith" — but he took quick action to rebuke the evil spirit and restore the cleansed boy to his father.

You may already begin to see trouble brewing here. We have three apostles feeling very special for having been chosen to go up the mountain with Jesus (and you can be sure they told no one that Peter had put his foot in his mouth with his inappropriate suggestion), and we have the other nine apostles being reprimanded by the Lord for their failure. Shouldn't the next scene be a group encounter in which in honesty and transparency they would all confess their limitations and reestablish group harmony? Alas, this was not to be. Rather, we find them arguing with one another about which of them was the greatest! Luke then tells us that Jesus stood a little child beside him to teach them that "he who is least among you all—he is the greatest" (Luke 9:48). Allegiance to Jesus was best demonstrated by those who welcome a little child in his name.

Evangelical Elitism

Perhaps to exonerate himself and also make sure Jesus knew how effectively his disciples had been serving him, John then told Jesus that they had seen a man driving out demons in Jesus' name and "tried to stop him, because he is not one of us" (Luke 9:49). Notice any irony here? Apparently the unnamed exorcist was succeeding in this ministry in Jesus' name to such an extent that the apostles couldn't stop him. Here are disciples of Jesus who failed to cast out a demon from a little boy, now admitting to trying to stop someone else who *was* having success. Personal jealousy may have motivated their attempt, but more likely it was group prejudice—John expected Jesus' approbation because the man was an outsider. Instead Jesus said, "Do not stop him, for whoever is not against you is for you" (v. 50).

Evangelical elitism is a serious spiritual disease. We tend to segment Christendom, label each division, and then proclaim anything or anyone that does not wear the label "evangelical" to be un-Christian. My experience in circulating in denominational and independent groups, Protestant and non-Protestant, has convinced me of three truths: (1) the true church of Jesus Christ can be found among members of all branches of Christianity; (2) all branches, including evangelicalism, have members who are very likely not disciples or even believers; (3) all branches suffer from an elitist disease. If the whole church were a professional sports league, we'd see churchmen jumping around with their index fingers raised and boasting, "We're number 1." Even if particular denominations do not believe they are God's only children, they are surely convinced that he values them most.

> If the whole church were a professional sports league, we'd see churchman jumping around with their index fingers raised and boasting, "We're number 1."

Evangelicals are not alone in suffering this disease, but they are often the quickest to deny it or not even think of it as a malady.

The next event on the journey carries a similar warning against elitism. Going through Samaria to prepare for the ministry of Jesus there, the disciples were flatly rejected by the Samaritans. James and John then volunteered to call down fire from heaven to destroy them. The text simply says, "But Jesus turned and rebuked them" (Luke 9:55), although some manuscripts add, "You do not know what kind of spirit you are of, for the Son of Man did not come to destroy men's lives, but to save them."

In both of these episodes Jesus taught his followers that his kingdom was far broader than they knew, and that their own tolerance was far narrower than it ought to be. Soon these lessons would be very important, because Jesus planned to recruit and train seventy-two other disciples for a special mission to the trans-Jordan region (see chapter 8, "Demonstrating the Gospel").

Three Would-Be Disciples

Three new candidates for discipleship are introduced in our text. To each of them Jesus gave a very stern word, and his comments add to our understanding of intensity as a kingdom quality.

Neither Foxes nor Birds

The first man came as a volunteer to Jesus: "I will follow you wherever you go" (Luke 9:57). Matthew tells us that this man was a scribe, a teacher of the law. While many of the scribes opposed Jesus, others were attracted to him. Most likely this man led a rather comfortable life, which prompted Jesus to reply, "Foxes have holes and birds of the air have nests, but the Son of Man has no place to lay his head" (v. 58). This seems to be an odd reply to someone who came with an unconditional offer of allegiance. Why would Jesus respond like this? We can only speculate, but it would not seem farfetched to assume that Jesus expected this scribe to have a hard time with the rigors of the outdoor accommodations that Jesus and his disciples accepted as part of their itinerant lifestyle. Perhaps the comforts of home would hinder this man's discipleship.

Does this contain a message for us? It may. A careful reading of the demands of discipleship that Jesus gave here and in other passages teaches us that material comfort, security of home living, and the traditional "good life" must not take priority over the work of the Lord. When we consider that the Lord's Great Commission is for his people to evangelize the world, it cannot possibly be right that Christians are huddled so comfortably in the West while thousands of population groups have yet to hear of Christ. In far too many areas the gospel light is barely a flicker.

Having been raised in a missionary denomination, I frequently heard the appeal for young people to give their lives to overseas service, yet I heard many of my friends say, "My folks want me to serve the Lord, but *not* on the mission field." Could it be that world evangelization has been retarded because so many would-be disciples are addicted to material comforts?

You may be wondering, "Does this mean God does not want us to have comfort, security, and the good life?" No, it does not mean that at all; rather, the converse is true—God does not want comfort, security, and the good life to have us. If these concerns master us, then Jesus cannot. No one can serve two masters.

Jesus' reply about foxes and birds contains an interesting hidden message. T.W. Manson shows that the Jews frequently referred to their enemies, the Edomites, as foxes, and to the Gentiles as birds of the air.[11] To this mainline Jewish scribe—a member of the establishment—Jesus was saying that his followers must not live by heathen standards. The Edomites were the descendants of Esau, who forfeited his birthright to Jacob for a pot of stew. Although Esau's birthright entitled him to the blessing of being a Jewish patriarch, material satisfaction meant more to him. Jesus was implying that the Israel envisioned by God will be motivated by spiritual drives, not material comforts. Choosing material comfort over spiritual achievement has held back many people from true discipleship.

A young man whose story is told in Mark 10:17-23 was such a person. Like the three would-be disciples in our text, this man seemed to have an appetite for spiritual things, so he asked Jesus what he needed to do to inherit eternal life. First Jesus pointed him to the commandments, which the young man said he had always obeyed. But then Jesus said, "One thing you lack. Go, sell everything you have and give to the poor and you will have treasure in heaven. Then come, follow me." This was too much for the man to take. "He went away sad, because he had great wealth." Perhaps Jesus was even more sad when he said to his disciples, "How hard it is for the rich to enter the kingdom of God" Because we will be learning more about the danger of materialism in chapter 11, let us move on to consider the second would-be disciple.

Let the Dead Do the Burying

Unlike the other two fellows, this candidate for discipleship was personally recruited by Jesus. The other two were volunteers, but to this man Jesus gave the same call he gave to Peter,

James, John, and others in the Twelve: "Follow me." We dare not press the point too far, but I am glad that both volunteers and recruits are represented here. Trying to build theology on innuendo and to tuck truth into tight packages is so tempting. Were it not for this recruit, I can imagine someone using this text to sermonize about how all those who hear "Follow me" do follow, while people who try to come on their own initiative do not. The fact is, we do not know what became of these three men. It might be inferred that they were discouraged by the severity of Jesus' words, but the text does not imply that, nor does it show a distinction between the response of the volunteers and this recruit. Matthew reports that this man already was a disciple (Matthew 8:21), but whether he continued to follow Jesus we do not know.

We do know, however, that he said to Jesus, "Lord, first let me go and bury my father." Because this does not seem to be an unreasonable request, we are shocked to hear Jesus reply, "Let the dead bury their own dead, but you go and proclaim the kingdom of God." Again, we are surprised to see Jesus dealing so harshly with a potential disciple. If his goal was to increase the number of disciples to assist him in proclaiming the kingdom of God (which is strongly suggested a few verses later in Luke 10:2), surely Jesus could have been more diplomatic. He might have taken lessons from some of our contemporary evangelists who will use any imaginable gimmick to get people to come to the front of the church, including an invitation to smell the flowers! Why was Jesus so stern and demanding? Had the man asked for this deferment because he wanted one last fling with his friends, we might better understand the tough line Jesus took, but burying one's father seems not only legitimate, but also honorable.

Some Bible commentators suggest that this man's father may not yet have died, so the request was not merely to attend the funeral. Most likely this was the oldest son in the family, and if the father was incapacitated and unable to care for the rest of the family, this son was expected to be the provider. If so, Jesus' response seems all the more severe. How are we to reconcile this with the mercy and compassion usually seen in Jesus?

Only one idea can adequately explain this, and it is summed up in the kingdom quality of this chapter: intensity. The mission of proclaiming the kingdom of God is so vitally important that all other human activities, relationship and responsibilities pale in insignificance. This is why on another occasion Jesus told a large crowd, "If anyone comes after me and does not hate his father and mother, his wife and children, his brothers and sisters—yes, even his own life—he cannot be my disciple" (Luke 14:26). Obviously Jesus did not expect this to be taken literally; he often used hyperbole to dramatize the importance of a concept. A fair interpretation is this: in comparison with the extreme importance and obligation of working for God's kingdom, even the strongest social allegiances will seem weak; even normal domestic relationships must be second in a disciple's affections.

Similarly, when Peter, needing reassurance about the value of following Jesus, said, "We have left everything to follow you!" Jesus replied: "I tell you the truth, no one who has left home or brothers or sisters or mother or father or children or fields for me and the gospel will fail to receive a hundred times as much in this present age (homes, brothers, sisters, mothers, children and fields—and with them, persecutions) and in the age to come, eternal life" Mark 10:28-30.

Why did Jesus in both of these passages use the family relationship to contrast with the mission of a disciple? Certainly it was because family responsibilities are *next in importance* to the work of the kingdom. Like the would-be disciple in our text, we need to understand our servanthood to God in this context. As important as family is, God's will is even more so. Reordering priorities with a "kingdom first" mentality is essential for any disciple of Jesus Christ.

Of course, caring for one's family is vitally important. Paul said, "If anyone does not provide for his relatives, and especially for his immediate family, he has denied the faith and is worse than an unbeliever" (1Timothy 5:8). But there are certain strategic occasions, though probably very few, when a special mission or ministry must be done at any expense. I am reluctant to say this because so many professional men of God have consistently neglected their families in favor of "the ministry." Our text needs to be understood in light of Luke 10, which describes the sending of seventy-two disciples on a very special mission. Jesus wanted all his followers to understand that proclaiming the kingdom of God was not something they should try to squeeze into their spare time. Nor could it be postponed indefinitely. The urgency of the work of the Lord demands a corresponding intensity by his followers. For those disciples who are prone to neglect their families, perhaps the key is discernment and honesty about whether it is Christ's mission or one's own ambition that is the motivating force. Gordon MacDonald's *Ordering Your Private World* has an excellent chapter on the difference between being called and being driven, which will be helpful for those struggling with this issue.[12]

Before leaving this recruit, we should try to understand the saying, "Let the dead bury their own dead." Although at face value the remark seems very insensitive, Jesus probably meant that of the many practical responsibilities claiming the attention of God's servants, some could be done as well or better by those not engaged in his service. The spiritually dead can attend to many of life's obligations that would impede a disciple on a mission. Paul admonished Timothy, "Endure hardship with us, like a good soldier of Christ Jesus. No one serving as a soldier gets involved in civilian affairs—he wants to please his commanding officer" (2 Timothy 2:3-4). This seems to be the same idea Jesus was communicating by saying that the dead should bury their own dead. There is a scarcity of people who are truly impelled and equipped to serve Christ, and far too many who lack motivation in that direction. Yet the latter are available to tend to obligations not related to God's kingdom.

This teaching is important for us today. With all the secular allurements and enticements available, we can so easily be sidetracked from our mission. We dilute our efforts, often with legitimate and wholesome endeavors. Having righteous intensity virtually guarantees that we will approach ministry like Jesus approached Jerusalem—with firm resolve and singleness of purpose.

A Farewell Party

The third would-be disciple in this passage came as a volunteer with only one minor condition: He wanted to go home and say good-bye to his family before joining Jesus. Even so, he received the most stern comment of the three: "No one who puts his hand to the plow and looks back is fit for service in the kingdom of God" (Luke 9:62). Undoubtedly Jesus detected in this man a hidden agenda or attitude that would hinder his effectiveness in ministry. The man used two words that indicate he was not good disciple material: "But first." He had it completely backward; already he was telling the Lord what he intended to do, clearly revealing a "me first" attitude. No wonder Jesus confronted him right away, telling him he was not "fit for service."

> The man used two words that indicate he was not good disciple material: "But first."

This may seem to be a severe criticism, but consider the motives and danger of going home to say good-bye. One possible motive may have been a desire for recognition. Being a disciple of a renowned rabbi could merit some lavish praise, which a self-absorbed person would not want to miss. Jesus may have seen in this man an unhealthy dosage of pride that was already derailing him from the tracks that led to kingdom living.

There was also a danger in returning home for a farewell. Friends, family, or a girlfriend would certainly have tried to talk the man out of his intention to take on the rigors of itinerant living. Many young people have gone off to Bible college in obedience to the call of God to prepare for missionary service, only to go home between semesters or after their first year and be dissuaded from continuing. Jesus knew this man would be susceptible to such influences.

Jesus also wanted to impress on this volunteer the extreme urgency of the mission. Sentimental send-offs are nice when one is going into the military or away to school, but the journey Jesus and his men were about to embark on was so important that it made such good-byes inappropriate.

The metaphor Jesus used was perfect. Plowing a straight furrow demands total focus on only that purpose. Holding the plow with one hand and turning your head and waving to the folks on the porch of the farmhouse will leave the field looking like a maze. What farmer would hire a worker who couldn't concentrate enough to plow straight? Why should the Lord take a disciple who has other priorities that override the work of the kingdom?

The prophet Elisha provides a good illustration of the attitude the Lord wants to see (1 Kings 19:19-21). Elisha was plowing with a yoke of oxen when Elijah found him. Since the Lord had previously told Elijah that Elisha was to be his successor, Elijah put his cloak on Elisha, a symbolic way for a prophet to designate a disciple. Elisha responded by asking if he might first go to kiss his parents good-bye. Sounds like the fellow in our text so far, right? But Elisha's attitude was very different. Not only did he kiss his folks, but he also slaughtered his oxen and used his plowing equipment as fuel for cooking the oxen as a meal for his family. Elisha's whole heart was in following Elijah, so he destroyed all evidence of his previous vocation as a statement that there would be no turning back for him. How similar to Bonhoeffer's statement, "The disciple simply burns his boats and goes his way."

No Volunteers, Please!

What application might all this have for us? The specifics will depend on one's life situation, but most of us should be able to recognize this text as a strong admonition about the intensity of our service for the Lord. Probably most of today's disciples serve in a church organization in some way. Perhaps we should examine how serious we are about that work. If we are giving less than our best—if we are looking away from the furrow—we are not fit to serve. As a pastor, I was often frustrated by church members who would accept as appointment but fail to do the work it entailed. Every position demands total effort, clarity of focus, and a righteous intensity that says, "Full speed ahead!"

One time I expressed this frustration to an elder who was a faithful and diligent servant of the Lord: "Why is it, Bob, that out in the world of business, people seem to take their responsibilities much more seriously than many people do in the church? Do we have to put up with mediocre service because church members are volunteers?" Bob responded quickly and with a good bit of fire in his voice, "There are no volunteer jobs in the Lord's work. Christians are *called* to serve and should be held accountable to the highest standards of excellence." Gaining that perspective has taken me a while, so conditioned had I been to the volunteerism concept, but I am convinced that Bob was right. Jesus said it as clearly as possible—a person who does less than his best is not fit to serve God. Recently, I heard a powerful quote: "Intentional mediocrity is sin."

Discipleship Principle #7: Focusing on Priorities

What are the lessons we learn from the three would-be disciples? From the first, we learn that being a disciple demands a proper perspective on material comforts and security. From the second, we learn to refuse to be drawn into other ventures that will weaken our effectiveness for the kingdom. From the third, we learn to give nothing less than our best in our service for the

Lord. In other words, focusing on kingdom priorities reflects the character quality of intensity, which helps us fulfill Discipleship Principle #7:

Discipleship Principle #7
Discipleship demands singleness of purpose, which is demonstrated by a sense of extreme urgency for advancing God's kingdom.

Chapter 8

Demonstrating the Gospel: Courage

Luke 10: 1-24

Discipleship Principle #8
Because the mission of the kingdom of God is accomplished by demonstrating and proclaiming the gospel, when courageous disciples further that mission, they *are* the kingdom.

For the most part, Jesus directed his efforts toward instilling character qualities, not ministry skills, in his followers. But the work of the kingdom has not been accomplished mostly by quiet, passive ascetics with sterling character; the church has always needed active, aggressive disciples to carry out its mission. In the first part of Luke 10, we see Jesus preparing his men for vigorous spiritual combat. It is one of the few recorded occasions where Jesus gave how-to-do-it instructions.

The kingdom quality this mission demanded was courage. At least seventy-two disciples were being sent into the heat of front-line battle against the powers of sin. They were going as soldiers of the kingdom of God to as many as thirty towns, places that Jesus himself planned to visit. Two-by-two he sent them "like lambs among wolves." Their weapons were words and deeds: proclamation and demonstration of the gospel.

Both/And

For many decades, one of the most intense debates in Christendom has centered on the nature of the evangelistic task. One segment of the church, usually considered the more liberal, has insisted that our job is to demonstrate the gospel through social action. This agenda calls for feeding and housing the poor, educating the illiterate, cheering the elderly, assisting the handicapped, and championing minority causes. Spending money to send Western missionaries to Third World countries has been denounced as colonialism. Instead, applauded have been the efforts of anyone who expresses humanitarian concern, regardless of creed. In fact, Christians of this persuasion are convinced that compassionate activity is the very reason the church exists.

It is certainly not difficult to locate Scripture passages to support this *demonstration* aspect of evangelism. A very popular one is Matthew 25:31-46, where we find Jesus' teaching that the ones to be invited into his kingdom are those who have fed the hungry and thirsty, welcomed strangers, clothed the naked, cared for the sick, and visited the imprisoned. They are "the righteous" who inherit "eternal life." Anyone failing to show this kind of compassion is cursed and will be told to depart "into the eternal fire prepared for the devil and his angels," a place of "eternal punishment." These are the words of our Lord, and surely the case for demonstrating the gospel could not be made stronger.

Evangelists of the *proclamation* school are usually more theologically conservative. They insist that the gospel is primarily Good News—a message that must be told, understood, and embraced personally and spiritually. Feeding hungry stomachs, they say, will do nothing for the soul, for Jesus did not die to give temporary relief to empty stomachs but to offer eternal redemption to sinners. Better, they add, to die hungry and saved than live healthy but damned. For them, any demonstrating of the gospel merely sets the stage for proclaiming its message of salvation. Scriptures for this point of view can also be marshaled. For example, to affirm evidence of his messiahship to John the Baptist, Jesus told John's disciples to tell him what they had seen and heard, namely "The blind receive sight, the lame walk, those who have leprosy are cured, the deaf hear, the dead are raised and *the good news is preached to the poor"* (Luke 7:22, emphasis added). We might expect the last statement to be that the poor are provided for, or fed, or given money, or in some way ministered to materially. But apparently their real need is to hear the gospel proclaimed.

It ought to be obvious to Bible students that we do not have an "either/or" situation here; we have a "both/and." The gospel must be *both* demonstrated *and* proclaimed. Works without faith are vain (Ephesians 2:8, 9); faith without works is dead (James 2:26).

Mission of the Seventy-Two

Our text in Luke 10 is fascinating because it shows Jesus training an expanded group of disciples. We know by studying earlier parts of Luke that by this time there were twelve who were firmly committed to Jesus and multitudes that enjoyed hearing him. But it is almost surprising to find such a large number as seventy or more being trained to do the kingdom work—especially against the backdrop of Luke 9, where we find Jesus' responses to three would-be disciples. The implication is that none of the three could "cut it," the demands of discipleship being so severe. We can therefore assume that these seventy-two were highly dedicated and qualified. Even with this large number, the Lord's first demand was that they pray for more workers because "the harvest is plentiful" (v. 2).

Jesus' plan had been set forth in Capernaum. When the people begged him to stay there, he said, "I must preach the good news of the kingdom of God to the other towns also, because that is why I was sent" (Luke 4:43). His instructions to the seventy-two were straightforward, yet challenging. They were to "travel light": no purse, bag, or extra sandals. They were to avoid all distractions, not even stopping to chat with folks along the way. When they entered a house, they were to give a typical Semitic blessing to establish a feeling of fellowship and openness. They were to remain where they were welcomed, eating what was offered. Their task was to "heal the sick...and tell them, 'The kingdom of God is near you'": (v.9). Whenever their ministry was rejected, they were to go out into the street and wipe the dust off their feet as a symbolic repudiation—a warning that people would be held accountable for rejecting the kingdom of God.

That was it! No further instructions. Perhaps because they had already seen him do it, no one asked, "Lord, exactly how are we to heal the sick?" No technique is given, no special words, no ointments, no formula, no ritual, and no prayer—simply, "Heal the sick." Yet the seventy-two were successful, for they returned joyfully saying, "Lord, even the demons submit to us in your name" (v. 17). Jesus' response gives us some insight into the reason for such simplified training: "I have given you authority." In other words, their ministry was an extension of his.

Miracles Today

Are miracles possible, or even desirable, in today's church as a way to demonstrate the gospel? This issue has been fiercely debated, and the current discussion about "power evangelism" and signs-and-wonders theology has the potential to polarize Christendom even further. Within the past few decades, the debate about miracles has left the church in disarray.

Catholics and Anglicans have rediscovered the healing ministry of the church and blown the dust off the liturgical formulae for use in special services. On the other hand, some fundamentalists and dispensationalist Protestants insist that the present-day manifestations of healing are fraudulent, because such gifts died with the apostles.

Although mainline liberal Protestants have rediscovered the healing ministry of the church, they have redefined "healing," restricting it to its naturalist aspect. Pastors and chaplains are now part of the "healing team," along with doctors, nurses, psychologists, and social workers. And, no doubt, God uses them.

Pentecostals and charismatics insist that healing is a vital part of the church's work, and the lack of it is due to weakness of faith.

Meanwhile, generic evangelicals don't know what to make of it all! They are uncomfortable with the theology and excesses of Pentecostalism, but they are equally disturbed by the theology and God-limitations of dispensationalism. They are baffled by the Anglo/Catholic approach and mistrustful of the liberals' disbelief in anything hinting of supernaturalism.

Obviously, the issue will not be resolved here. The reason that consensus may never be reached is partly theological and partly political. People do not like to surrender their dearly held prejudices, especially if it means capitulation to the other side. Note those last two words: "other side," for that may be the hub of the problem. Too many Christians continue to view others within Christendom as the enemy. As long as we continue to divide the camp by inadequate and damaging labels—and as long as the question is not "What is true?" but "Who else believes it?"—the church will continue to be a noisy gong and a clanging cymbal. Have you ever listened carefully to orchestra instrumentalists warming up prior to a symphony? Their individual skills are evident, but the chaos of the collective sound is discordant and annoying. That is the church on the issue of miracles today.

Other than criticizing other arms of the church and defending our own theology and practice, is there a way out? Can the church come together on this issue? Can Christendom become a symphony (meaning "one sound" from Greek)? Probably not. The stakes are too high for those with vested interests. But perhaps it is possible to present a constructive statement that contains some hope for reconciliation. The idea is not to get every musician playing the same instrument or the same notes, but following the same piece of music under the directions of the Master Conductor. Here, then, is a view of the role and possibility of modern miracles:

The occurrence of a miracle was considered by the Jews to be a sign that God was sanctioning the activity of the agent of the miracle. Thus, Jesus used miracles (the Apostle John called them "signs") in the promotion of his spiritual kingdom. When he left earth, only about 500 Jews believed that he still lived and that the kingdom would proceed. The best "proof" of his resurrection, the best apologetic to convince the Jews of Jesus' claims had to be the continuation of the miracles in his name. This was not to be a substitute for saving faith but a catalyst for it, as we see in the Book of Acts. These having been done and recorded historically, no need remained for these "apologetic" miracles; hence, the disappearance of them in Acts. Apostolic miracles continued for a while, but the thrust of the gospel was carried forth through the body-life of believers in local house churches. This does not rule out miracles today, but there is a distinction in purpose. In the early church, miracles were done almost indiscriminately as signs of the continuing power of the risen Messiah. Today, while miracles are still occurring, they are done as sheer acts of grace. Charismatic gifts are tied to the meaning of charis – grace. The individual, not the kingdom as such, is more the focus of today's miracles.

(For further discussion about this, see my book, *Walking in Your Anointing*.)

This statement will not satisfy all Christians, perhaps not even most, and not even me. There may be some cultural aspects to this issue that defy even this fairly broad outlook. It seems that God is more often doing sensational miracles in so-called "third world" areas than in more "advanced" societies. Nevertheless, besides expressing an outlook on God and the Scriptures that enables us to avoid either contextualizing the miracles of the first century or denying their possibility today, this statement affirms the full sovereignty of God, respects the historical distinctives in the plan of God, embraces the whole of Scripture, and allows for mystery in a world that is not merely naturalistic. It also escapes the simplicity of formula-ism and avoids imposing false guilt and embarrassment over ineffectiveness. Furthermore, it leaves the church with a mission of compassion that is totally dependent on ministering "in his name."

It must be emphasized, however, that this statement was not developed for pragmatic or even reconciling purposes, but in an attempt to be faithful to the Scriptures and present day realities. Such basic motives as these have great potential for promoting harmony in the body of Christ if Christians are willing to drop their more selfish agendas.

Show and Tell

What is the mandate of modern disciples? Assuming that both demonstration and proclamation are needed to communicate the gospel effectively, how are we to proceed? Because for hundreds of years Christians have not been able to command miracles like the seventy-two did, we have had only a tell-it gospel with little to show. A preaching-only gospel is not convincing to much of the world, nor should it be. That would be like trying to sell a car with a beautiful body but no engine.

The fact that using miracles for evangelistic purposes seemed to pass off the scene fairly early in the church's life ought to give us some hope and a clue, for the church continued to succeed without such supernatural attestation. What was its strategy? The primary power of the early church lay not in supernaturally endued individuals, but in its corporate kingdom lifestyle. This principle has been stressed in several chapters of this book, but nowhere is it more germane than here.

Corporate Christianity

The early church, with its Jewish cultural background, was not nearly as individualistic as Christianity is today. Because the Christian life was experienced corporately, almost communally, the church became an alternate culture that was a showcase for the values of the kingdom of God. There was no need for superstar evangelists or fanatical zealots. The testimony of a community of disciples of Jesus Christ living in harmony, worshiping in reverential awe, ministering with compassionate love, and courageously embracing their enemies was powerful enough to convince a skeptical world of the reality of Christian truth. Evangelism in those days was a by-product of a church body that lived what it believed. There were no evangelism committees, no video or DVD series, no special seminars or crusades, not even any pocket-size booklets for personalized soul-winning. Not that these things are useless, but when they become substitutes for the community kingdom living to which the church is called, they are concessions to failure.

> The church became an alternate culture that was a showcase for the values of the kingdom of God.

The Apostles Teaching

Being devoted to the **apostles' teaching** implies that the people learned together and recognized the apostles' authority to instruct them in important matters. What were the apostles teaching? Undoubtedly their subject was what Jesus spoke about most often—the kingdom of God. We know this was fresh on their minds, for Acts 1:3 tells about the post-resurrection ministry of Jesus to the apostles in which "he appeared to them over a period of forty days and spoke about the kingdom of God."

This text does not mean Jesus was talking about heaven, but about kingdom living on earth. Neither was he giving theoretical lectures in theology. Jesus' teaching about the kingdom was always relational and ethical. Because he addressed the human will as well as the mind and emotions, Christ showed the apostles how to live together and how best to witness in his name. The apostles had earlier learned that unity among believers would convince the world that Jesus did, in fact, come from God the Father (John 17:33). And, indeed, it was the early Christians' communal caring that caught the world's eye. The references to "one another," which appear so frequently in the Epistles, indicate the strong relational element woven through the apostles' teaching. The entire church body, not just the individual, was their concern.

The apostles were disciplers, not merely teachers. We ought not to think of them as adult Sunday-school teachers, but as spiritual mentors. Their mandate was to communicate "likeness," as Larry Richards calls it.[13] They were known as men who "had been with Jesus" (Acts 4:13) and were living examples of the Master's statement that "everyone who is fully trained will be like his teacher" (Luke 6:40). The goal, as expressed by Paul, was spiritual maturity: "the whole measure of the fullness of Christ" (Ephesians 4:13).

Fellowship

While persisting in the apostles' teaching gave the early Christians the theological and sociological framework for functioning as a kingdom community, activating those principles in daily life required **fellowship** (*koinonia*), a very deep level of sharing and caring. This sort of camaraderie or *esprit de corps* is possible only in a minority group that views itself as possessing a sacred and solemn mission. When personal ambitions and prerogatives are willingly sublimated for the sake of a common cause, a sense of responsibility for the well-being of the group is shared not just by its leaders, but by all the members.

The body imagery that Paul used in 1 Corinthians 12:12-26 is an apt expression of Christian fellowship; it implies total integration and interdependence of the parts. Christians were involved with each other spiritually, financially, professionally, domestically, and socially. This demanded an intense commitment and an extraordinary level of trust. Since the apostles had already learned to live this way as a micro-community, the model for the early church's life of fellowship went right back to the hills and roads of Galilee.

Breaking the Bread

The focal point of the life of fellowship was the love feast, the Lord's Supper, which may have been celebrated daily or weekly. Simply called "**the breaking of bread**," this meal was partly memorial, partly mystical, partly communal, and partly eschatological. The believers remembered their Lord's death and enjoyed his presence, horizontally as a social group and vertically in worship. While this was not a public meal and therefore not demonstrably a witness to unbelievers, the reputation Christians gained as a classless society came mostly from this weekly gathering. This is why Paul was so deeply concerned that the participants should wait until all were present before the meal began.

Slaves were not always able to be punctual, but Paul would not tolerate any hint of their being considered second-class citizens in the community (see 1 Corinthians 11:33-34).

"Breaking the bread" probably implies more than the Lord's Supper; it was undoubtedly a time of community worship of the living Lord. Even though early Christians in Jerusalem continued going to the temple (Acts 2:46), their worship of Christ was more likely in the context of their love feasts. The centrality of worship services in the life of the early church is seen in the frequent references to the sense of awe and reverence surrounding them.

It is important to understand that this worship, like that of the Jews, was a corporate activity. Private worship is important, but corporate worship is imperative. God delights in the gathering of his people in worship; indeed, he dwells in the midst of their praises (Psalm 22:3). In speaking of corporate worship, we are referring to more than congregational worship as we experience it today. Sometimes (usually?) congregational worship is nothing more than a group of people engaged in private worship in the same place. We are self-conscious, not body-conscious; passive individuals, not active participants in a shared experience. Such worship can never be a demonstration of God's kingdom to non-Christian attenders. It is just another religious program. But when congregational worship is active, involving, communal, dynamic, and reverent, it is truly corporate and a sign of the community of the King. A divinely charged community of believers who live and worship in corporate unity and fellowship is the best demonstration of the truth of the gospel.

Prayer

What makes this kind of corporate unity possible is **prayer**. Through prayers of praise and thanksgiving, the presence of God is most poignantly sensed. Through prayers of confession and mutual burden-bearing, fellowship is best maintained. Through prayers of supplication, discernment and guidance are forthcoming. Through prayers of intercession and petition, total kingdom concern is experienced. Corporate prayer is foundational to kingdom community, and the early Christians knew the importance of tenacious praying. In fact, this is one of Jesus' kingdom strategies, and we will consider it carefully in the next chapter.

Discipleship Principle #8: Demonstrating the Gospel

Obviously, there are other ways to demonstrate the gospel besides corporate kingdom living. Throughout the centuries, many heroic individual deeds have been signs of the kingdom, just as testimonies of transformed lives are powerful validations of the gospel today. Parachurch ministries have done much to expand the influence of Christianity around the world. But God's primary instrument for establishing the kingdom of God is his church, which is most effective when believers employ Discipleship Principle #8:

Discipleship Principle #8
Because the mission of the kingdom of God is accomplished by demonstrating and proclaiming the gospel, when courageous disciples further that mission, they *are* the kingdom.

Chapter 9

PRAYING TENACIOUSLY: DEPENDENCY

Luke 11:1-13

Discipleship Principle #9
People of the kingdom place their full confidence in the goodness and power of God, continually depending upon him for provisions, forgiveness, guidance, and spiritual strength.

Here is a strange paradox: Jesus prayed. During his earthly ministry, the eternal Son of God, who lived continually with his Father in intimacy and who possessed all the power of deity, was frequently seen to pray. If he always knew the Father's will, was always in communion with him, and could always provide whatever was needed, why did Jesus pray?

The complete answer to that question is beyond our grasp. In the mystical union of the Godhead, there is much that remains incomprehensible to finite man. In a more simplistic sense, however, we *do* know why Jesus prayed. He wanted to. Wherever relationship runs deep, communication is precious, intimate, and inevitable. The bond between the Father and the Son made prayer the most natural and reasonable of all Jesus' activities on earth. Part of the mystery of the Trinity is that the God-man had the ability to be completely autonomous, yet he continually lived dependently in union with his Father.

Visual Faith

Have you ever watched someone who was earnestly praying? It is a powerful experience. As a young boy who would occasionally get up very early, I would always find my mother sitting in her chair, completely absorbed in prayer. Other times I would wake up in the middle of the night, aware of a light in the family room, which was adjacent to my bedroom. There would be my dad, who was not a good sleeper; but he was a good pray-er. Those experiences impacted me deeply. When we see someone in earnest prayer, we are watching mystery. Something very private and personal is occurring—the deepest kind of communication between the human soul and its Source.

What must agnostics think as they watch someone praying? Full attention and devotion are being given to someone unseen. The pray-er obviously believes that there is reality to what he or she is doing and that it is worthwhile. The skeptic must conclude that either the person is self-deluded or a reality exists about which the skeptic knows very little. It must be like a dog seeing a human work a computer.

At least five passages in Luke's Gospel speak of Jesus praying. On one such occasion, after a very busy day of ministering to people, Jesus went out at daybreak "to a solitary place" for communion with the Father (4:42; cf. Mark 1:35). We are also told that he would often slip away into the wilderness to pray (5:16). Prior to selecting the twelve apostles, he went off to the mountain and spent the whole night in prayer to God (6:12). His prayer on the Mount of Olives shows how he struggled in prayer shortly before his arrest (22:41-44). The text for this chapter, Luke 11:1-13, begins by saying that the disciples were watching Jesus pray and then they asked him to teach them how.

146

Praying was an integral part of their Judaic tradition, so why would these young men ask for further instruction?

The text says that they wanted to be taught to pray, "...just as John [the Baptist] taught his disciples." While prayer was certainly a rich part of Jewish heritage and family life, apparently the disciples of both John and Jesus saw in their teachers an attitude toward prayer that was totally new to them. Perhaps the Twelve saw an intensity, persistence, and earnestness so far beyond their own experience that they knew Jesus' way of praying somehow related to the wisdom, power, and perspective they saw in him. Their request was not only an expression of their admiration for their Master, but an indication of their own spiritual hunger. Because they were not aware at this early stage of how central prayer would be to their later ministries, they were probably not looking for a trigger to empower their efforts. They were simply asking to be taught how to pray because they knew Jesus enjoyed a relationship with God for which they also yearned.

"Father"

The disciples' motivation was right, and it was rewarded. They wondered whether they could have a relationship with God similar to that which Jesus enjoyed. The answer came in the first word of the prayer they were taught: "Father." As often as these men had prayed and heard prayers, this was likely the first time they heard God addressed so personally and intimately. The disciples were being taught that the basis for prayer was not God's status as Creator ("Almighty God of the universe..."); nor was it as the Deity of the patriarchs ("Great God of Abraham, Isaac, and Jacob..."). Prayer, Jesus taught, was to be based on the personal Father/child relationship. "When you prayer, say, "Father...."

Jesus undoubtedly used the common Aramaic word for father, "Abba," which denotes an intimate family relationship. It was the filial term of respect used by a trusted, mature son who understood his role as an heir; it was not a term used by a young child. The English word *Daddy* is not adequate, since it lacks the reverence that comes with adult understanding.

We have a hard time appreciating what saying "Abba" meant to the disciples. Jewish traditionalists would consider it impious and unfitting to speak to God or about God with the same term used of an earthly father. The Pharisees might refer to God as Father, but they used "Abba" to suggest greater distance in the relationship. The difference Jesus brought was not so much in our understanding of the nature of God, but in our relationship to him. Jesus was teaching his followers that—as sons of God—they have the stature of mature, trusted confidantes.

Some who read this book have had a male parent who poorly modeled fatherhood. Christian counselors often see people who have difficulty relating with God because of their negative experiences with inadequate father figures. They must then redefine fatherhood by looking to the character of God, rather than rejecting the term. This reprogramming process may not be easy or painless, but our heavenly Father is eager to help.

Those of us who are fathers have an awesome responsibility. A major part of the real-life theology of our children will develop from the meaning we impart to the word *father*. Perhaps that is why the apostle Paul gave direct commands to fathers about their parenting (Ephesians 6:4; Colossians 3:21).

A Pattern of Dependency

The kingdom quality featured in this chapter is dependency, and nowhere is this attitude more clearly defined than in the Lord's Prayer. Fortunately, the disciples asked Jesus *how* to pray, not what to pray, because the Lord's Prayer is very brief and focuses mostly on the five aspects of our dependency on God. (You have probably noticed that Luke's version of the prayer is shorter than the more familiar one in Matthew 6:9-12.) Jesus was providing a pattern that expresses an attitude, not necessarily the words, we are to use whenever we pray.

"Hallowed Be Your Name"

We have already seen that the first way we are dependent on God is for *relationship*. Addressing him as "Father" affirms that we are to relate to him in a spirit of intimate fellowship. But just as surely as God is "Father," he is also the Holy One, the Most High whom we must worship. "Hallowed by your Name" tells God that we honor him with the reverence that acknowledges his sanctity, power and glory.

"Hallowed" means sacred, or holy—altogether distinct, set apart, unique, wholly "other," and worthy of profound reverence. "Hallowed be your name" has found expression in many ways in the history of the people of God. Moses was told to remove his shoes in God's presence; Isaiah spoke in wonder, "Woe is me," when he recognized God's presence; Ezekiel and John (Revelation 1:17) fell on their faces as dead; Peter (Luke 5:8) said, "Go away from me, Lord, I am a sinful man;" Thomas uttered in fear, "My Lord and my God," when he beheld the resurrected Son of Man. During the dedication of God's temple under Solomon, the priests and Levites could not continue to minister, so overwhelming was the glory of God filling the temple. Gideon, Jacob, Hagar, and Manoah all feared that they would die because they had "seen" God.

Nevertheless, when we pray, we usually jump right in with "Dear God, bless this and bless that. Do this and do that.... Amen." C.S. Lewis says we treat God as our cosmic bellboy, lacking all sense of who God is, of his eternal and awesome attributes, lacking perspective on the incredible privilege of being able to speak in the presence of ultimate and supreme royalty. Some years ago, Queen Elizabeth II visited the United States. One day the papers reported the *faux pas* committed by a woman who ventured to speak to the queen without being bidden to do so. Respect for earthly royalty is a matter of social protocol. Respect for the King of kings should come naturally but is often lacking.

Words are not necessarily important in God's presence. They are like blips on a screen monitoring the heart. What is *in* the heart is the only significant aspect of our part in prayer. The most meaningful prayer I have ever heard began this way: "Father... [long, long, long pause; then with trembling voice]... hallowed be thy name." This was not staged for dramatic effect; it came from a reverent soul with a true, albeit limited, understanding of God's character.

"Your Kingdom Come"

The words *Father* and *hallowed be your name* establish the nature of our relationship with God. The next phrase, "Your kingdom come," deals with the second area of our dependency: *perspective*. How are we finite, flawed, self-centered creatures to know what is truly important and why we are here? God has given us enough intelligence and curiosity to realize that these questions matter. Presumably, the common earthworm and even the "higher" animals are not bothered by questions about meaning and value. But, because we are created in God's image, humans have deep longs for significance and permanence. God has left us answers for this craving, for he is a God of revelation. He has spoken to us, and his Word tells about his plan, expressed in both the Old Testament concept of "covenant" and the New Testament concept of "kingdom." The kingdom is the covenant consummated, which is why Jesus taught us to pray, "Your kingdom come." Disciples of Jesus crave to see God's kingly reign in full authority in every arena of life. The alternative is the world of evil, sin, and death. Right now we live in the tension of both kingdoms. God's kingdom is here and now, but not fully; it is also then and there.

Craving God's kingdom shows that we understand what God is doing, what his plan is, and what part we are to play. Craving

God's kingdom reveals that we have God's perspective on life. It shows that we desire heaven on earth. The prayer for God's kingdom is quickly followed in Matthew's version by a parallel thought: "Your will be done on earth as it is in heaven." If we yearn for God's will to be done, we want all sin and its consequences to be banished. By asking

> Craving God's kingdom reveals that we have God's perspective on life. It shows that we desire heaven on earth.

God to exercise full and complete authority in every slice of life at every moment, we express our dependency on him for making right what is wrong. We acknowledge that neither human government, social reformers, philanthropic agencies, nor even the church can bring about all the earthly improvements we desire. This perspective positions all the rest of our prayer life in a properly dependent mode.

"Give Us Each Day..."

Up to this point the pattern for prayer has mentioned our dependency on God for relationship and for perspective, but now we come to our petition for material *provision*: "Give us each day our daily bread." The emphasis on "each day" and "daily" may have been intended to remind the disciples of how God provided for the Israelites during their wandering in the wilderness. Some of the people were not content with gathering only a day's supply of bread ("manna") and soon found that if they tried to hoard more, it spoiled. Others grumbled at the monotonous fare, so God provided meat as well. As we know, bread is "the staff of life," the symbol of survival, if not necessarily our favorite food. This may be why Jesus chose bread to represent his broken body. A piece of the Passover lamb might have been more appropriate to memorialize his sacrifice, for he was already known as the

Lamb of God, and the Israelites traditionally slaughtered a lamb to atone for sins. But lamb is not universally available; bread is.

In our modern culture our dependence on God for food is not so evident. We go to the supermarket where acres of food are on display, already processed and attractively packaged. We can buy a week's supply, take it home, and store it in refrigerators and cupboards, knowing we can go back to the store at any time and buy more. We rarely consider the farmer's role in producing the food, let alone God's provision. People in the first century and those in less-affluent cultures today understand the prayer for daily bread far better than we do. In one sense we enjoy great freedom in knowing that abundant food awaits our purchasing power. On the other hand, in our apparent independence we lose the sense of God's constant loving care for us.

"Daily bread" should be understood to mean more than our next meal. Jesus was instructing his people to learn to trust God to supply all our material needs. (We will consider this more closely in chapter 11, as we focus on the character quality of contentment.) It is important that we recognize our ultimate dependency on God, even in a world of plenty. One way to acknowledge this is by showing our gratitude in the age-old practice of saying "grace" at the meal table.

In today's frantic pace of life, many families find little time to share meals together. Eating is rarely a communal activity that invites fellowship. If we eat on the run or in front of the TV, we miss one of the most important times for family bonding. Even when Jesus was preaching to the masses, he stopped preaching at mealtime, took time to organize people in smaller groups, and made sure they ate in a leisurely fashion. He began those meals by thanking his Father for the food. (See, for example, Mark 6:39-41.)

When we plow right into a meal without pausing to thank God for this blessing, we reveal that we are ungrateful, independent-minded, and undisciplined. Our physical urge is overruling our spiritual sensitivity.

A story is told about a Christian who was meeting a nonbeliever for a business lunch one day. When the food was served, the Christian bowed his head and silently thanked God for the meal. His guest was embarrassed (or convicted?) by this and said rather indignantly, "I don't bother with that religious stuff. When my meal comes, I just dig in." The Christian paused and answered, "Yes, well, that's just what my dog does." We may question the tactfulness of that reply, but it does point out an interesting thought. A human being who fails to see the provision of daily bread in a spiritual context is denying an important part of his or her humanity and acting like an animal.

"Forgive Us"

We also depend on God for *forgiveness*. Both our moral "mistakes" and our deliberate sins testify to our rebellion against God and our failure to love our fellow humans. Sinfulness not only saddens God and injures others; it also affects the sinner in a negative way. People who never request forgiveness carry an ever-increasing load of guilt. If their conscience becomes so scarred that they no longer perceive their guilt, they begin suffering physical consequences. Romans 1:29-31 amplifies this thought clearly, showing how unforgiven people who reject God degrade their bodies and corrupt their minds:

> *[They are] filled with every kind of wickedness, evil, greed and depravity. They are full of envy, murder, strife, deceit and malice. They are gossips, slanderers, God-haters, insolent, arrogant and boastful; they invent ways of doing evil; they disobey their parents; they are senseless, faithless, heartless, ruthless.*

A life without forgiveness is shadowed by the dark cloud of sin. Joy, freedom, and peace become transitory at best. Most parents can recall times when their young children had done something forbidden. How miserable the little one would be until the misdeed was revealed and he or she was forgiven by Mommy and Daddy! That is a natural feeling, and honest adults realize they never outgrow it. Our sins block open fellowship with God and others until we confess them and are forgiven.

Forgiveness costs. It is never free. And, ironically, the one who forgives pays the price. In the case of God's forgiveness, Christ paid the cost by his death. No other way exists. We cannot make restitution through our own efforts. If I slander a brother and even if I later ask his forgiveness, he will continue to pay the price of a damaged reputation, even though my accusations were false. In gaining forgiveness we are totally dependent upon the injured party. It is our responsibility to ask for forgiveness, but only the offended one can grant it.

The importance of reconciliation in human relationships is emphasized by the second part of the petition: "...for we also forgive everyone who sins against us." Jesus taught that our relationship with God is closely related to our dealings with other people. When we choose not to forgive those who have harmed us, God is not obliged to forgive us, regardless of our confessions. The parable of the unmerciful servant in Matthew 18:21-35 makes this abundantly clear. No mercy to those who show no mercy, says the parable, and so says the Lord's Prayer.

"Lead Us Not..."

Finally, in Luke's version of the Lord's Prayer, we express our dependency on God for *protection and guidance.* Because we realize that temptations, trials, or testings will attack where we are most vulnerable, we ask God to spare us from our own weaknesses. As the Lord's followers, we need to know that he will not lead us into situations where our downfall is inevitable. The Lord tells us, through Paul that, "...God is faithful; he will not let you be tempted beyond what you can bear. But when you are tempted, he will also provide a way out so that you can stand up under it" (1 Corinthians 10:13).

Matthew's version of the Lord's Prayer adds, "...but deliver us from the evil one." Forgiveness of a previous sin does not mean we are henceforth insulated from the same sin or other kinds of sin. We need to be led out of the way of temptation and delivered from the enemy of our souls, who delights in trapping God's people in sin and severing their fellowship with the Father.

To summarize: In this short prayer Jesus teaches us to express our utter dependence on God for:

- A right relationship with him ("Father...hallowed")
- A proper perspective on life ("Your kingdom come")
- Daily provision ("Give us")
- Forgiveness ("Forgive us")
- Protection and guidance ("Lead us not")

Each of these petitions admits that we cannot make it on our own, that we need God. We are his children, and he wants us to continue to be childlike in our dependency on him. God requires humility, which is expressed in dependency, and God hates pride, which oozes from haughty conceit. Therefore, he loves the gratitude that follows rewarded dependency and despises the arrogance that proclaims self-sufficiency.

Persistence

After giving the prayer—our pattern of dependency—Jesus emphasized the importance of persistence in prayer (Luke 11:5-13). A short parable got the point across. A man who has received an unexpected guest at midnight finds himself in an embarrassing position of having no food to offer. Proper hospitality is exceedingly important in the Middle East, even today. Rather than allowing his guest to go to bed hungry, the host goes to another friend to borrow some bread. At first he is turned down: "Don't bother me. The door is already locked, and my children are with me in bed. I can't get up and give you anything." That answer does not satisfy the petitioner, so he keeps knocking until his friend on the inside gets up and gives him what he needs—"because of the man's boldness [or persistence]" (v.8).

A similar illustration is found in Luke 18:1-8. Jesus told this parable to his disciples "to show them that they should always pray and not give up" (v.1). In this case a widow kept appealing to an unsympathetic judge for justice against her adversary. Her persistence finally paid off, for the judge reasoned within himself, "Even though I don't fear God or care about men, yet because this widow keeps bothering me, I will see that she gets justice…" (v.4-5).

Both parables might be confusing because they seem to imply that the responses to the petitions are given reluctantly. Is God like the sleeping friend who does not want to give bread to his friend because it is so late in the night? Or is God like the unsympathetic judge who gives justice to a widow only to get rid of her? Obviously not, in both cases. We need to remember that parables are not exact allegories; that is, it is not legitimate to interpret them by finding correspondence to reality in every detail of a story. Parables usually teach only one lesson. Here the lesson speaks not to the nature of God, but to the importance of persistence.

A word of caution is necessary here: Delays are possible! I get impatient with road improvements. To the sign that says "Slow Men at Work," I usually give a sarcastic "Amen." But one such warning caught my attention and gave me more patience with a highway delay: "Temporary Inconvenience for Permanent Improvement." I'm still rather skeptical about the "permanent improvement" part, but the idea made a lot of sense to me, and I think we need to take that same mentality into our prayer life. God often delays giving us immediate answers to our prayers so he can turn temporary inconveniences into permanent improvements. Frequently, especially in our novice days as pray-ers, we do not first try to discern God's will before petitioning him. Seasoned pray-ers do not rush into God's presence with their wish list. Learning to meditate or contemplate on God's Word and his ways will save us from much fruitless asking.

Evelyn Christenson, whose books on prayer have probably helped more people around the world in our generation to improve their praying than any other books, suggests that we learn to pray questions rather than answers. I think she means that unless we are sure of God's will, we should approach God with inquiry rather than insistence. The question, "God, how does this situation fit in with the rest of your plan, and what will best advance your kingdom?" is more appropriate than supplying our own answer: "God, here is what I want you to do about this." Only God knows why he delays in any given case, but here are a few ideas that should give us more patience and persistence in prayer; six reasons for God's delay in answering my prayers.

First, sometimes God wants to stretch my faith. I may naturally tend to despair when I do not get an answer, but God wants me to know that he will not be a slave to my timetable. He is teaching me to submit to his schedule and remain strong in faith while I wait.

Second, God wants me to become truly dependent on him. If I received answers quickly all the time, I would never be brought to the point of desperation where my only hope is in God. If he answers while I am still comfortable, I may never learn to be fully dependent on him.

Third, God may choose not to give a quick answer because he knows how easily I can dismiss his work as coincidence. Even though I bring the matter to the Lord, when the answer comes quickly I tend not to believe that God has been the cause of my good fortune. This happened to a group of believers who had been praying for Peter the night before his scheduled trial and possible execution (Acts 12:1-17). After Peter's miraculous escape, he came to the house where they were meeting, but they would not believe the servant girl who answered the apostle's knock. They even conjectured that perhaps it was Peter's angel, so skeptical were they that God would answer their prayer.

A fourth reason why God may delay answering prayer is that circumstances are not right for the answer. He surely knows better than I whether what I request is good for me, and whether the timing is best. I can think of times when he has spared me from certain disaster by not answering my prayer promptly. (Of course, as many insightful disciples have pointed out, God *always* answers prayers—but sometimes his answer is "NO!".)

A fifth factor for God's delays is the strength of the evil one. After unsuccessfully trying to heal a demon-possessed boy, the disciples were told by Jesus that only fasting, prayer and sufficient faith would prevail in such a case (Mark 9:14-29; Matthew 17:14-20). To be sure, the enemy cannot withstand the will of God, but we are engaged in spiritual warfare, and Satan will not give in without a struggle.

The sixth reason God delays answers is to increase our gratitude when his response finally comes. When I get instant gratification, I rarely show adequate gratitude, I think that I must have deserved a positive answer, or that God was obliged to grant my petition. Some years ago our family spent a summer on a Caribbean island where riding motorbikes was customary. My youngest son intensely wanted to have a ride with me, but I would not grant his desire immediately. After weeks of waiting semi-patiently, he was rewarded with a ride and was incredibly thankful for it. The rising anticipation made him all the more grateful when my positive answer came. Learning to accept God's timing while we persist in prayer is a step toward spiritual maturity.

The Role of Faith

Persisting in prayer demands a generous measure of faith, no question about it, but some Christians assume that the amount of their faith determines whether or not God will give them the answer they want. In one of his sermons, Stuart Briscoe discussed the role of faith in the life of prayer by using the analogy of wintertime ice. He said you can have a great deal of faith in the ability of ice to hold your weight, walk out onto it, and end up very cold and wet. The amount of faith will not help in the least if the ice is thin. Conversely, you may have very little faith in the ice, walk gingerly on it, and be held firmly because it is three feet thick. Your limited faith was rewarded because it was placed on a solid object.

The amount of our faith may be irrelevant; the focus of our faith is key. When we depend on systems and objects that do not merit our faith, we are usually sorely disappointed. In the spiritual realm, people often put faith in false religions and think they are forever secure. But they have invested their faith in "thin ice," in something

> It is infinitely more important to know our great God and invest even a little faith in him than to put enormous faith in anything or anyone else.

that cannot provide eternal life. It is infinitely more important to know our great God and invest even a little faith in him than to put enormous faith in anything or anyone else. Rather than trying to build up the amount of our faith, we would be wiser to spend the effort getting to know and understand God better, for the more deeply we know him, the greater we realize he is. As we gain greater appreciation for his majestic glory, his infinite wisdom, and his boundless love, we automatically exercise more faith in him.

Discipleship Principle #9: Praying Tenaciously

Our God is a loving Father who wants our relationship with him to be characterized by dependency and the belief that he is more than adequate to meet our needs. He also wants us to be tenacious in our praying, being confident that he will answer according to his good time and will. As we grow in our life of prayer and dependency, we will be modeling Discipleship Principle #9:

Discipleship Principle #9
People of the kingdom place their full confidence in the goodness and power of God, continually depending upon him for provisions, forgiveness, guidance, and spiritual strength.

Chapter 10

SPEAKING HONESTLY: TRANSPARENCY

Luke 12:1-12

Discipleship Principle #10
Because disciples believe that the kingdom of God is the realm where truth prevails, they strive to have honest and open relationships.

P eople in the real-estate business say the three most important factors in buying property, whether land or buildings, are location, location, and location. In Bible interpretation (or "hermeneutics," the technical term), the three things we most need to know are context, context, and context. The key question in interpreting Scripture is: How does the passage being studied relate to the surrounding verses? Someone has said that a text without its context is merely pretext.

Context is truly important in the passage before us. Luke 12 would be extremely difficult to understand if we did not have the background of Luke 11. The New International translation begins chapter 12 with "Meanwhile..." The New American Standard Bible more accurately says, "Under these circumstances," giving greater emphasis to the context found in chapter 11. What were those circumstances, and why are they important to our understanding of Luke 12:1-12 and its teaching about the kingdom quality of transparency?

A Generation of Woe

The dramatic events in Luke 11 form the apex of Luke's account of Jesus' life prior to the events of Holy Week. As the contrasts between Pharisaic Judaism and the kingdom of God are drawn more starkly by the ministry and teaching of Jesus, the Pharisees intensify their attack. Some of them even suggest that his power comes from Satan (Matthew 12:24; cf. Luke 11:15), perhaps the ultimate blasphemy. Jesus has a few things to say about them also. A large portion of Luke 11 strongly denounces the scribes and Pharisees and their generation.

Seven times Jesus refers to the people of "this generation" (Luke 11:29-32, 50-51), condemning them for not responding to his miraculous ministry while clamoring for more signs, and for bearing the same disposition of their fathers, who had murdered the prophets of old. "This generation" will be condemned by the Queen of the South, who sought out Solomon's wisdom" (v. 31), "and by the men of Nineveh, who repented at the preaching of Jonah" (v. 32). "This generation" will also be held accountable for the bloodshed of all the martyred prophets (vv. 50-51). Moreover, Jesus pronounces six "woes" against the Pharisees and scribes, condemning their hypocrisy, pride, corruption, elitism, murderous disposition, and false teaching (vv. 42, 43, 44, 46, 47, 52). Apparently Jesus does not plan to run for office on the Pharisee ticket.

As the clouds of conflict thicken, thousands of people rush to catch the action, even trampling on one another to watch what promises to be an exciting fight. They see trouble brewing and do not want to miss seeing the Pharisees "getting theirs" at last. No one has ever confronted the Pharisees like this!

Bad Bread

"Under the circumstances," Jesus turned his attention to his disciples and gave them the teaching in Luke 12:1-12. In this volatile moment, any other leader or teacher would have been looking after his own well-being. Not so with Jesus. Perhaps the depth of his commitment to training his disciples is seen nowhere more clearly than here. He turned a moment of extreme danger into an object lesson for his followers. (That's almost like the pilot of a crashing jet explaining the law of aerodynamics to his co-pilot!) Jesus never allowed his foes or the crowds to dictate his agenda. It was time for discipleship class, so Jesus began the lesson! "Be on your guard against the yeast of the Pharisees, which is hypocrisy" (v. 1b).

All of Jesus' criticism of the Pharisees stood on one common factor: They lived a lie. Their dishonesty infected every area of their lives. Jesus, who said, "I am...the truth," did not want his followers to pattern their lives after these deceitful religious leaders. So he warned the disciples by using the imagery of "yeast," or leaven.

Leaven is not used for its flavor, but for its effect: It causes bread dough to expand or rise. If you have ever seen or eaten unleavened bread, you may remember that it appeared flat. For the Jews, unleavened bread was a symbol of their national identity and uniqueness. During the night of the exodus from Egypt, Moses had instructed his people, to pack unleavened bread, perhaps because there was no time to wait for the leavening process (or simply because the flat bread would take less space in their backpacks). From that time forward, Jewish people have eaten unleavened bread during Passover, known also as the Feast of Unleavened Bread. Some Christian churches use unleavened wafers for Holy Communion to continue the symbolism. This serves as a reminder that we are pilgrim people not living in the land of our true citizenship. We are always in exodus on our journey to God's Promised Land, his kingdom.

163

Although the effect of yeast on bread is desirable, Scripture pictures leaven as a potential evil in two ways. First, leaven corrupts. Jesus saw that the influence of the Pharisees was corrupting Jewish society by false teaching (e.g., Matthew 16:6-12). Similarly, Paul, alarmed because the Corinthians were tolerating a church member living immorally with his own stepmother, wrote, "Don't you know that a little yeast works through the whole batch of dough? Get rid of the old yeast that you may be a new batch without yeast..." (1 Corinthians 5:6-7).

Second, leaven puffs up, giving an outside appearance of substance that does not really exist within. Like "whitewashed tombs," another image Jesus applied to the Pharisees (Matthew 23:27), leaven creates a deceptive exterior. Thus, leaven provided an apt image for corruption and dishonesty. Perhaps you remember your parents' warning about not telling lies, not even "little, white lies." They probably explained that you can't tell just one lie; someone will catch you and then you will have to tell another lie as a cover-up. And so it continues, until you get into a habit of telling lies. In today's society we can no longer assume that all parents, teachers, employers, and other authority figures are champions of truth. In fact, children and young people are often encouraged to compromise truth (i.e., lie) for self-serving purposes. For example, I know Christian parents who helped their teenage son lie about his age so he could get a job. They justified this by saying they wanted him to earn money for college so that he could serve the Lord!

In politics, too, we assume that we rarely get the truth, and we don't even expect it. Richard M. Nixon resigned his presidency in disgrace partly because of the citizenry's outrage at his lying about the Watergate incident, but many believe he was so ruthlessly and relentlessly exposed more because the media did not like him than because of his dishonesty. Some people still say his only crime was getting caught, and that Watergate and the related cover-ups were just normal political activities. The public outcry over other politicians' personal or public immorality has been healthy, but their acts are usually viewed as "indiscretions," not sins against God and the electorate. It is not too surprising, then, that attorneys, though pledged to serve justice, often devise ways of fogging the truth or presenting only half-truths (is there such a thing?).

In the marketing and sales arena, even Christians have been heard to argue that there is absolutely nothing wrong with letting a customer continue with an overinflated view of a product's merits, as long as the salesperson did not actively contribute to that false impression. "Buyer, beware," the rule of the marketplace, is seen as sufficient justification for tolerating this subtle form of deception.

We cannot blame only business leaders, politicians, attorneys, and salespeople for the erosion of truth in our culture. Self-serving deception is rooted deeply in all of us. Even people in the church succumb to the temptation to project themselves as far better than they know to be true. The pressure to appear holy, spiritual, mature, or just "together" tempts us to be modern Pharisees. A friend told me recently about a recovering alcoholic who had found this to be true in a church-based support group. My friend said to me, "Basically, the recovery group he's now in are people who have really been through the pits. The 'ordinary Christians' weren't able to hack it. They weren't able to be that honest. To the drug and alcohol addict, they tended to say, 'It can't be that bad. All you have to do is...' And they were unwilling to reveal any flaws or deep needs in themselves." Among Christians there is a great tendency to be judgmental, and this goes hand-in-hand with a lack of transparency. As we have already seen, being judgmental is directly tied to the inability to face the truth about ourselves (see chapter 5: "Examining Myself").

The church ought always to be in a place where truth—honest, vulnerable, transparent truth—is held in highest reverence. And perhaps it would be, if we Christians were less judgmental of others and more willing to repent and confess our own sins. An unleavened church would surely express the character of God's kingdom as God wants it to be.

Leavened Leaders

Leaven is an apt metaphor to illustrate the dramatic effect of corruption on its environment. The metaphor is all the more effective because bread is part of daily life. Spelled out clearly, the admonition of Jesus was to beware of the defiling influence of spiritually flawed people, especially those in positions of leadership.

The leaven of the Pharisees was "hypocrisy," by which Jesus may have meant one of two things. First, we note that on many occasions Jesus denounced the Pharisees for being false leaders who cared little for the people, but gloried in their own position. The statements in Luke 11 provide condemning evidence of this hypocrisy, a key idea being: "...you load people down with burdens they can hardly carry, and you yourselves will not lift one finger to help them" (v. 46). In contrast to Jesus, who consistently ministered pastoral care to his flock of followers and many others who reached out to him, the Pharisees seemed to delight in adding to the cares of their followers by making religion more rigorous and demanding.

Charles Stanley, pastor of First Baptist Church in Atlanta, speaking to a group of ministers about pastoring from the pulpit, said, "Shepherds don't beat sheep; they feed sheep." Many pastors, unfortunately, view the pulpit as a shield or bunker from which they can wage warfare, shooting fiery arrows or hurling grenades at the harried church members under their "care." Jesus wants his disciples to minister sympathetically, not to use their leadership role for prideful, self-serving purposes. Shepherds are to guide and nurture others.

A second reason Jesus warned his disciples about the leaven of the Pharisees was to protect them from naively assuming that these religious leaders would have their best interests at heart. On the contrary, the disciples would need to exercise great discernment and caution. Jesus predicted that the Pharisees would pursue the followers of Jesus, using every piece of evidence and every whisper to condemn them. Jesus himself later fell victim to their duplicity, their cunning lies and twisted truths. They told the Jewish court that Jesus had claimed he would tear down the temple and rebuild it in three days and that he taught people to disregard the laws of Moses. They testified to the Romans that Jesus claimed to be a rival king to Caesar and that he was inciting insurrection among the Jews. Lest his followers be deceived by the respected position and apparent piety of the Pharisees, Jesus warned them to "Be on your guard."

No Secret Christians

Notice also in this passage that Jesus said the disciples should not fear the Pharisees or try to hide their activities or disguise their message. Rather, they should go on boldly with their witness, recognizing that only God has final authority over a person's destiny. They were not to fear even martyrdom. What they were to guard against was disowning the Son of Man. In a prophetic mode, Jesus told the disciples that all they said and did would be made known to the Pharisees. What they thought was concealed would be made known. What they thought had been said in secret would be brought before the Jewish tribunal because their witness for Jesus would threaten the religious establishment. This being so, the disciples would need to be both truthful and courageous. This is central to the kingdom quality of transparency.

We saw in chapter 8 that the kingdom quality of courage is needed if we are to serve Christ by demonstrating and pro-claiming the gospel. The related quality of transparency—sheer, clear truthfulness—may also require extraordinary courage, since one's very life may be in jeopardy when speaking the truths of God's Word. Imagine for a moment that you live in a country where all Christian activity is monitored and that you suspect your church meeting place is bugged by electronic surveillance devices or being reported by planted government agents. Occasionally, some of your members disappear. How would that affect the ministry and fellowship in the church? Would you be inclined to stand and give a testimony?

Many Christians in the first century and even today have faced such persecution. Some, out of fear, have disowned Jesus; some of them have later repented and been forgiven, as promised in Luke 12:10. Many others have faithfully confessed Christ at peril of their lives. Those who have paid that awesome price are witnesses in the most profound, literal sense—the Greek word for witness being "martyr." History tells us that all the apostles except John died as martyrs. But church leaders were not the only ones who cherished truth more than life. The historian Sulpicius Severus wrote in his *Chronica* that after Nero's torching of Rome in A.D. 64, in order to escape the blame that was obviously his, Nero accused the Christians and declared open persecution on them.

> *...the opinion of all cast the odium of causing the fire upon the emperor, and he was believed in this way to have sought for the glory of building a new city. And, in fact, Nero could not, by any means he tried, escape from the charge that the fire had been caused by his orders. He, therefore, turned the accusations against the Christians, and the cruelest tortures were according afflicted upon the innocent. Nay, even new kinds of death were invented, so that, being covered in the skins of wild beasts, they perished by being devoured by dogs, while many were crucified, or slain by fire, and not a few were set apart for that purpose, that, when the day came to a close, they should be consumed to serve for light during the night.*

Jesus was certainly not referring to human torches when he told his disciples, "Let your light shine before men" (Matthew

5:16), but truly those Christians were "the light of the world," and through their witness Rome and its colonies were Christianized.

Training in Transparency

Few Christians in the West are likely to be physically persecuted for their faith, for now. But the anti-Christian sentiment that is growing in the United States is a threat at the same time as we find most disciples to be spiritually soft and unfit. We have not often had to take a stand for Christ requiring us to be truthful under pressure. We might like to think that we would be faithful under even the most extreme of conditions, but we cannot know that for sure. Are you certain that you would not renounce Christ if your life were threatened? Because most of us have not had training in such spiritual combat, we cannot predict how we would respond.

God set up a place to prepare us to work on our transparency so that we will be able to witness courageously. It's called the church. That's right; the church is the place for spiritual training. If we learn to be transparent within the fellowship of believers, we will likely be forthright and honest in any situation. The Epistles frequently admonish us to be open and sincere in our relationships within the church. If we wear masks when we are with those who believe as we do, we are unlikely to be honest and courageous before those who despise Christian truth and have the power to persecute us.

Jesus gave other reasons for transparency besides preparing to testify truthfully in a hostile environment. The primary reason is that God's very nature is truth, and as his children we should imitate him. Some might complain that God has veiled himself from us, so how can we possibly consider him to be transparent? In a word: incarnation. God has revealed himself fully in Jesus Christ. He who is the eternal Spirit became mortal flesh by the most transparent act ever.

Another reason God wants us to learn transparency is that honesty undergirds all other kingdom qualities. People who refuse to be known on an intimate level have an impossible time loving and receiving love because love is based on trust. The depth of any relationship is proportional to the degree of trust between the parties. When we hide ourselves from another, we reveal a lack of trust in that person. A degree of privacy is

> Revealing may be risky, but remaining closed is hazardous to our spiritual health.

necessary at times, but our first instinct should be transparency. To model Christ, we must always strive to be trustful and self-revealing.

Transparency within the Christian community also keeps us properly humble. Because God "opposes the proud but gives grace to the humble" (James 4:6), transparent relationships must characterize his church. In fact, the church cannot truly be the body of Christ unless honesty reigns. We must be a confessing community, openly acknowledging both our individual sins and our shared beliefs. The word *confess* literally means to agree with or speak together the same thing.

The church is healthy to the extent that we speak honestly to one another for mutual support. A person with a well-developed spiritual gift of mercy, for example, can help a less sensitive prophet see the need for speaking the truth "in love;" the prophet, on the other hand, can teach the merciful one how to speak "the truth" (Ephesians 4:15). Many Christians do not recognize their own spiritual gift because they have not revealed themselves to others in the body on a deep level. If spiritual gifts are not known, they will not be used effectively, and the entire church is the poorer for it.

Of course, revealing ourselves to one another is risky. In one of my first MasterWorks groups, Sam (fictitious name) revealed something personal that another member must have mentioned outside the group. After a few weeks of wondering why Sam no longer came to our meetings we discovered he was angry and hurt that his story had been leaked. That will happen occasionally, but the answer is not to withdraw and clam up. Instead, we must lovingly confront our own and others' weaknesses and keep growing in grace. Because Sam separated himself from the body of Christ, today he is shriveling up spiritually. Revealing may be risky, but remaining closed is hazardous to our spiritual health.

Old Testament "Baptism"

Naaman, commander of the Syrian army, was highly regarded by the king as a valiant warrior. But, like all of us, Naaman had a flaw; he was a leper; (see 2 Kings 5). Although Naaman undoubtedly hoped to deal privately with his flaw and thereby keep his dignity intact, the prophet Elisha's prescription for him demanded that he humble himself by dunking in the Jordan River seven times. Naaman protested, saying that Syria had better rivers than Israel (it seems like we all know better than God how to deal with our flaws!) Little could Naaman know the symbolism of those Jordan waters. Centuries later, thousands of Jews, including our Lord, would go to those same waters to humble themselves in baptism.

Naaman was eager to be healed of his leprosy, which he saw as his only flaw. He was blind to his greater defect; pride. God dealt with Naaman's pride by requiring that he be dunked in the Jordan. Because those of us who avoid transparency may regard other problems as more serious, we may be surprised to find God wanting to deal first with the pride that causes us to be less than honest with ourselves and others.

The symbolism of baptism includes cleansing, the gaining of greater transparency. As I write, I am looking out a window clouded by dirt that will not be removed without conscious effort. A dirty window may cause social embarrassment, but intentional clouding of the soul is far more serious, for it deprives one of God's primary strategy for confronting both the world and the church with the fullness of the gospel—the honesty and humility of God's people.

171

Full Disclosure

What is the best way to develop transparency? Surely, learning to tell ourselves the truth about ourselves is a good beginning point. When we honestly confront our own pride, selfish ambition, lust for power, anxiety about comfort and security, self-righteousness, and need for admiration, our shell of superficiality begins to crack. Our very brokenness begins to yield the spiritual fruits and humility and transparency. (Dr. Larry Crabb has written excellently about honesty in *Inside Out*.[14])

Notice the radical saying in Luke 12:2, "there is nothing concealed that will not be disclosed, or hidden that will not be made know." What did Jesus mean by this saying? We might at first be inclined to interpret it eschatologically, that is, to assume Jesus was warning his followers that every word they say will be made known publically in the time of judgment, so they had better be careful about their speech. Perhaps our confusion about this verse arises because the same idea and words are found in three other New Testament passages: Matthew 10:26, Mark 4:22; and Luke 8:17.

The context of Matthew 10:26 parallels our text, Luke 12:2, but the next verse is worded differently. In the Matthew version, Jesus clearly instructs his disciples to speak in daylight what *he* told them in the dark, and to proclaim from rooftops what *he* whispered in their ear. They should not be afraid of the consequences. Although they might be killed for their honest discipleship, this would be preferable to being disowned by the Father in heaven because they had concealed what Jesus had taught them.

The other two passages in Mark 4 and Luke 8, parallel each other within the context of not hiding a lamp under a bowl or a bed. Instead, the light is put on a stand, because whatever is hidden should be disclosed. Since both passages follow the parable of the sower, Jesus seems to be telling his disciples not to limit their fruitfulness by concealing their true selves.

How do we disguise or hide ourselves? Our text in Luke 12 implies that we often put on disguises by speaking falsehoods; or we hide the truth by merely keeping silent. Jesus was aware that the primary reason we lack transparency is fear, but even fear of death does not excuse our covering the truth. The context shows that Jesus was concerned about both falsehood and silence. On the one hand, his followers must not be like the Pharisees, whose "leaven" included false teaching; on the other hand, his disciples must be willing to confess him aloud, for their silence would be the same as denying him.

The Real Macho Man

One of the worldly tendencies toward which men are particularly prone is artificiality. Men often try to project a culturally defined image instead of revealing God's work-manship—our real, humble self as it is transformed in Christ. Men think that it is not "macho" to be vulnerable. A real man, we've been told, is aggressive and invulnerable and has no soft, "feminine" feelings. Emotions are for women, we say. We wear a "tough guy" mask, call it masculinity, and preserve our shallowness and superficiality. In reality, such hiding is blatant cowardice that keeps us from becoming involved with others and their weaknesses under the pretense that we ourselves are strong.

For some reason, appearing self-sufficient is very important to most men. Much of our so-called masculinity is tied to the idea of strength – physical and otherwise. Any sign of weakness is seen as undermining our manhood. This is one reason why religion is far more popular with women than with men. Religion implies a sense of need, an ability to own up to our weakness and dependency. It requires petition, adoration, humility, caring, and other expressions of emotion that seem threatening to many men because they expose our weaknesses. Most of us Christian men have much to learn about true strength, the willingness to appear as we really are, secure in the knowledge that who we are in Christ is adequate.

Lies, Truth, and Consequences

Early in the life of the church, God dramatically demonstrated the importance of honesty in the affairs of his kingdom. Acts 5 tells the story of Ananias and his wife, Sapphira. It seems that Barnabas had sold a field he owned and brought the proceeds to the apostles for distribution to the many new Christians in need. Ananias and Sapphira, however, were neither as generous nor as honorable as Barnabas. They also sold property, but retained part of the profit, but acted as though they were contributing it all. Since they were under no obligation to donate all their property, they were not judged for withholding some of it; God's severe judgment fell on them because of their dishonesty. They were hoping to deceive the entire church by projecting a false piety, and in so doing they became dramatic examples of God's intolerance for religious duplicity.

Although no doubt many have tried a similar tactic and temporarily gotten away with it, Ananias and Sapphira did not. First, Ananias dropped dead when Peter confronted him with the sin; three hours later, Sapphira met the same fate. Both of them had "not lied to men but to God" (Acts 5:4).

By way of contrast, Acts 7 tells of the open honesty of Stephen, a man who was entirely transparent, even in the face of extreme danger. His situation was exactly as Jesus had been predicting in Luke 12. Because of the power of Stephen's witnessing, some of the Jews stirred up sentiment against him and brought him before the Sanhedrin, where false witnesses testified against him. Stephen seized the opportunity to declare boldly his understanding of God's working in history to send the Messiah. Then he courageously revealed his knowledge of Jesus as the Christ, whom his audience had betrayed and murdered but whom God had raised. Stephen's words were not popularly received. Yet, as his persecutors were stoning him, Stephen cried out, "Lord, do not hold this sin against them."

Perhaps you have noticed that Stephen suffered the same fate as Ananias and Sapphira. So how did his transparency benefit him? There is one big difference. God himself slew Ananias and Sapphira in an act of judgment, whereas Stephen, who was granted a vision of the glorified Jesus standing at the right hand of God, experienced a genuine martyr's death. Stephen certainly will be granted the special status of the martyrs mentioned in Revelation 6:9-11.

Nothing as dramatic will happen to most of us, but we, too, may be faced with the alternatives of confessing Christ or denying him. Our response in that moment is already being determined by the transparency we are willing to exhibit now. Most Christians have much room for growth in this kingdom quality. We are naturally more inclined to hide our true selves than to be completely honest. Transparency, however, is required in the church because it reflects God's nature, undergirds many other qualities of discipleship, and keeps us properly humble. The text we are studying looks outward, expecting that we will be called upon to be courageously transparent as Christ's witness in a hostile world. Such times may come in our lifetime, even in our religion-friendly culture. Remember, the society that crucified Jesus was not hostile to religion per se, but to the exclusive claims of Jesus, which demanded personal commitment.

Discipleship Principle #10: Speaking Honestly

As long as Christians remain complacently quiet about evil in our society and about the unique ability of Jesus to deal with sin, we will have no trouble in this world. But we will be seriously tested when we take a stand on a biblical principle that is opposed by a statue of the state, or when we attempt to proclaim our faith publicly or evangelize people of other faiths. To endure such testing, we need practice in transparency. Our churches provide that learning opportunity, which is exactly the point of Discipleship Principle #10.

Discipleship Principle #10
Because disciples believe that the kingdom of God is the realm where truth prevails, they strive to have honest and open relationships.

Chapter 11

Living Carefree: Contentment

Luke 12:22-34

Discipleship Principle #11
Sabbath and Jubilee principles, with their economic, social, and theological implications, must govern a disciple's everyday lifestyle.

Christians have a perplexing and difficult path to walk. Not only are we called to live according to a demanding ethical standard, we have other "handicaps" as well. We all would agree that for the sake of our testimony in the neighborhood, we Christians should keep our yards well groomed, our cars clean, and our houses in good repair. When do your non-Christian neighbors do these things? Mine do them on Sunday mornings. We should also be highly involved in civic and community functions, keep abreast of world events and the latest books, socialize outside the church fellowship, and spend plenty of time with our children. When do your non-Christian acquaintances do these things? Mine do them on weeknights, when I am often attending church meetings or serving the Lord in some other way.

Christians are the busiest people I know. We have more to do and less time to do it in than others, and yet we are supposed to be free of cares and anxiety. Jesus commanded us not to worry, and Paul reinforced that teaching (Luke 12:22-34; and Philippians 4:6). So now we worry about not worrying, but we hardly have time to practice not worrying!

Carefree

What comes to mind when you hear the term *carefree*? I think of a young child innocently enjoying the security of loving parental companionship during summer vacation—lying on a grassy bank with a fishing line in the river, or riding piggy-back on Dad's back, going from one amusement-park ride to the next. It's difficult to think of any adult experience that is completely carefree. With maturity come obligations and burdens, and Christians have the added responsibilities of discipleship. So what did Jesus mean by telling his followers not to worry?

First we must ask if Jesus himself had a carefree life on earth. Yes and no. Surely he took very seriously the cares of his role as suffering servant and soon-to-be crucified Messiah, so he could not have meant that we should try to escape the burden of our responsibilities. However, throughout his earthly life, Jesus lived free of the kinds of cares that grip most humans. He said that we, too, should not worry about material security: what we will eat, what we will wear, our life span, or our possessions (Luke 12:22, 25, 33). In short, we should be free of anxiety when it comes to the most basic human needs. Is that not strange advice? What is more important than our well-being and very existence?

What? Me Not Worry?

Two answers leap out from our text. First, if we broadly define "worry" as taking on ourselves responsibilities that God never intended us to have, we can see that by worrying we are claiming personal autonomy and ownership of our lives. But it is *God* who owns our lives, and he bears the responsibility to care for us. This is exactly what Jesus meant by pointing us to other parts of his creation. He said, "Consider the ravens." (The Greek word for "consider" means to scrutinize, or look at very carefully; John Stott suggests that this is God's command for all of us to practice his hobby of bird watching!) Birds are cared for by God, though they neither plant nor harvest fields. Jesus then reminded us that we are of much greater value to God than the birds.

He also told his followers to "consider how the lilies grow." God clothes them brilliantly, better than Solomon in his finest regalia, yet they bloom for a very short time and then are tossed into the fire with the grass of the field. God's children need not be consumed with worry about their clothes, for "Life is more than food, and the body more than clothes." Jesus' point is that God takes care of the important issues—kingdom living and eternal security. Surely he will also provide for our lesser concerns—the food and clothing we need for earthly comfort.

Christ is telling us that something holds far more importance than our physical welfare. We are to seek first the spiritual advancement, God's kingdom. His kingdom must take precedence over all else. The reason we can trust God to care for our material needs is that "your Father knows you need them" (v. 30).

Does this really make any sense today? Sitting in a Bible study or a church service when these verses are cited, we probably would not argue against the principle involved. But how can it work in our twenty-first-century, capitalist society? What happens to farmers who do not plant their fields? Does God miraculously fill their barns? What happens if no one spins thread to make clothes? Does God float down dresses and suits from above? Paul said that whoever does not work should not eat (2 Thessalonians 3:10). Did Jesus and his disciples never think about their next meal or never get new clothes? Was Jesus advocating a hobo or hippie lifestyle?

Let's go back to the text to answer those questions. First, notice that Jesus was speaking to people who *already* had a Father/child relationship with God. Although God is the Creator of the world and its people, he is not necessarily everyone's Father. Only those who become his spiritual children by the new birth can rightly call him Father. Those who are not yet spiritually alive do not have that security. Simple logic tells us that. Given God's fatherly care, Jesus told his disciples not to be anxious about daily needs. That did not mean they could be lazy and would never need to lift a finger to support themselves and their families. Rather, he was saying that those committed to the kingdom work of the Father could trust in his ongoing provision.

The Jubilee of Jesus

There is more at work in this passage than what is on the surface. The historical context of the text is very significant: Jesus was giving this teaching during Jubilee Year.

"Jubilee" is a word not found in the New Testament, but it is an essential part of Old Testament tradition, the life of Israel, and the teaching of Jesus. To understand how the idea of Jubilee could be part of Jesus' teaching, we first need some background.

After his baptism (when Jesus received divine affirmation of his relationship with his Father), and after his temptation (when he showed that he would not use his power for personal advantage), Jesus began his kingdom work as an itinerant preaching ministry. One of his first "pulpits" was in his hometown synagogue in Nazareth, a town held in scorn by most Jews. The Nazarenes were very independent in their outlook on life, probably because they lived along a major trade route and were exposed to many foreign influences. When Nathanael first heard about Jesus, he questioned whether anything good could come out of Nazareth (John 1:46). The year Jesus went public with his mission is debatable, but many scholars believe it was A.D. 26. Jesus was probably born in 4 B.C., so he would have been about thirty years old when he began his public ministry.

The service of worship and instruction in the synagogue at Nazareth was similar to that in all Jewish synagogues. First was the reciting of the Shema, the affirmation of belief in one God, which begins, "Hear, O Israel: The LORD our God; the LORD is one," from Deuteronomy 6:4-7. After the Shema, there would be a time of prayer, then a reading from the Law and from one of the prophets, and finally a message based on those readings. On his return to Nazareth, Jesus attended the synagogue on the Sabbath, "as was his custom" (Luke 4:16). He was handed the scroll of Isaiah at the time for the reading of the prophets. Jesus found Isaiah 61 and read it:

The Spirit of the Lord is on me,
because he has anointed me
to preach good news to the poor.
He has sent me to proclaim freedom for the prisoners
and recovery of sight for the blind,
to release the oppressed,
to proclaim the year of the Lord's favor. Luke 4:18-19

Apparently he read this passage with such intensity that after concluding the reading and sitting down, Jesus remained the object of rapt attention. All those present had their eyes riveted on him, as though expecting him to say something more. He obliged them by saying, "Today this scripture is fulfilled in your hearing?" – words that created a break with tradition. Knowing that the people would wonder how he was able to make such a statement, Jesus then challenged his fellow Nazarenes by contrasting the works of God in Old Testament days with their expectations for the present. Because they were doubtful that anything spectacular could still happen, they were skeptical about the reports of Jesus' ministry in Capernaum (see Mark 2). Jesus used two Old Testament examples to show how those who consider themselves to be God's chosen people were not always the ones who received God's grace. His audience was furious at the inference that their God might look favorably on Gentiles!

During the days of Elijah, when there was a great famine, the prophet was sent to a widow in the region of Sidon to minister to her needs. This woman was a Gentile, not a daughter of Israel. A generation later, Naaman, the captain of the Syrians and also a Gentile, was cleansed of leprosy through the ministry of Elisha. The Jews of Nazareth did not appreciate Jesus' tampering with their deeply held prejudices, so in a rage they led Jesus to a cliff, intending to throw him down. But Jesus escaped their evil intentions.

What specifically had upset Jesus' audience when he said, "Today this scripture is fulfilled in your hearing?" In Jewish theology, certain passages of the prophets were linked with related passages of the Law, much as theme-related Scriptures are linked in modern-day worship lectionaries. Isaiah 61, which Jesus read in the Nazareth synagogue, was always read with Leviticus 25, which gives instructions about the Sabbath Year and the Jubilee Year. Every Jew reading Isaiah 61 would understand that "the year of the Lord's favor" was anticipated in the Year of Jubilee.

For Israel, every seventh year was to be a Sabbath Year. The land was to remain fallow, or unplanted. After seven Sabbath Years—on the fiftieth year—in addition not planting the fields for a second successive year, three other things were to occur: debts were to be forgiven, slaves were to be liberated, and land was to be redistributed to the original family owners. Jubilee meant a total social reordering that fairly well abolished economic and class hierarchy. During Jubilee, while the latter three activities held consequences for specific parts of the population, *everyone* was affected by the injunction to let the fields lie fallow for a second successive year. This meant that the people needed to rely upon the providence of God to sustain them, which (besides allowing the land to rest) was clearly God's intention.

John Howard Yoder, in his book *The Politics of Jesus*,[15] shows that A.D. 26, when Jesus gave this teaching, was a Jubilee Year. Therefore, many of the teachings of Jesus about material security and depending on God for provision of needs were particularly pertinent to Jews who were being faithful to the Jubilee Year command.

An interesting Old Testament passage shows how serious God was about Jubilee Year. Jeremiah 34:12-21 prophesies the coming onslaught of the Babylonians. The prophet Jeremiah was told by the Lord that the immediate cause for the oncoming destruction of Judah was unfaithfulness to the covenant requirements for the Year of the Sabbath and the Jubilee Year. God wanted Israel to remain dependent on his blessings, and these commemorative observances ensured that dependency. In Jesus' day, Israel was more financially secure, but having to depend entirely on God to provide grain every seven years was a stretching discipline for the Jews.

The Fallow Year

What was Jesus actually saying to his contemporaries? And what implications might Sabbath Year living and Jubilee have for us? While the application of these covenant principles will vary from one culture to another and one century to another, they contain universal indicators of the amount of carefree dependency we can place on God. And therein lay contentment.

Jesus did not speak directly about leaving the land fallow as part of Jubilee Year, probably because the Jews were most faithful about following this command. Nevertheless, it took great courage to leave their fields uncultivated and unsown every seven years. No doubt many of them worried a great deal, as God had anticipated: "You may ask, 'What will we eat in the seventh year if we do not plant or harvest our crops?' I will send you such a blessing in the sixth year that the land will yield enough for three years" (Leviticus 25:20-21).

In A.D. 26, when Jesus referred to Jubilee Year in his message in the Nazareth synagogue, he was eager to reveal that the way of the kingdom of God, which he and his disciples would follow, was a continuation of the Jubilee principle in everyday living. Later, addressing his disciples, Jesus gave these words, which must be understood in a Jubilee context:

"Do not worry about your life, what you will eat; or about your body, what you will wear. ... For the pagan world runs after all such things, and your Father knows that you need them. But seek his kingdom, and all these things will be given to you as well" (Luke 12:22, 30-31).

Far from encouraging the disciples to become complacent, this teaching urged them toward a courageous and active lifestyle in which dramatic trust in God would be the hallmark of their existence. A rough paraphrase of Jesus' intention might be: "God expects you to work hard during the six years prior to Sabbath Year. If you do that, you can confidently obey God's command to rest the land for that seventh year, counting on him to take care of you. Go ahead and courageously leave your fields untilled. Just as God will continue to provide for the birds, which never sow or harvest, he will meet your needs if you set your eyes upon his kingdom. Notice that the Gentiles, who pay no attention to Sabbath Year, are not richer than you are."

The kingdom quality Jesus was teaching here is contentment, which removes all care for anxiety and self-striving. The God who creates is also the God who sustains. We acknowledge his sustaining power by relying on him in our daily routine. To be content, we must trust God and not question his goodness, omnipotence and purposes by worrying and trying to take back control.

You Deserve a Break

Living by God's economic principles, or according to Sabbath and Jubilee principles, means several things for

Christians. Certainly it means taking appropriate rest for ourselves. The principle of one day of rest per week may be even more important than ever. When Paul affirmed that no particular day is more sacred or holy than another, he was not negating the principle of Sabbath rest. God our Maker knows our need for rest and variety. We might wish we could be

> God our Maker knows our need for rest and variety. He commands us to relax and refresh our mind, body, and emotions by resting one day per week.

bright and alert throughout nonstop days and nights, but God has not made us that way. He commands us to relax and refresh our mind, body, and emotions by resting one day per week.

Taking a break from our weekday work routine is an important requirement for physical, psychological, and spiritual health. This principle has varied applications, of course. People who earn their living by physical labor certainly need a literal rest for their muscles, ligaments, and bones. Those of us who normally sit at a desk eight to ten hours a day might use the Sabbath to rest our minds and strengthen our bodies. Whatever way the principle of rest is applied, using some of that time to worship God and reflect on his goodness is still a valid command. The Jubilee concept guarantees that we can trust God to provide, so we do not need to risk burnout by trying to make a living seven days a week.

Need or Greed?

People who have the ability and opportunity to earn more than enough money to be financially secure are greatly admired and envied in our society. Some of them are generous with their possessions; many are not. Unfortunately, wealthy people may have everything they need except a proper sense of their place in the world. Even moderate affluence can so easily trap us into thinking we are rightful owners of what we possess. In truth, because God owns everything and we are his tenants (Leviticus 25:23), he will not allow anyone to be his competitor. People who refuse to acknowledge God's dominion, and who selfishly indulge in what they feel they have earned for themselves, are living contrary to the rules of God and are under his judgment. This is why Jesus made the startling statement that it is difficult for rich people to enter the kingdom of heaven (Luke 18:24).

The Jubilee principle calls us to live modestly, be generous with any surplus we may earn, and not make material wealth the focus of our existence. This is illustrated by the parable of the rich fool (Luke 12:13-21). This man had an abundance of crops. Rather than using some of his harvest to help others, he built bigger barns so he could store up more for himself and feel even more secure and self-satisfied than before. The Lord's rebuke was: "You fool! This very night your life will be demanded from you. Then who will get what you have prepared for yourself?" (v. 20).

Distinguishing between needs and wants is difficult in our consumer, media-hyped society. What was a "want" a few years ago is a "need" today. We so easily justify our materialistic indulgence by comparing ourselves with our more affluent neighbors and deciding that we need (and are entitled to) the same standard of life they have. God has promised that he will supply all our needs, not to give us everything we want. In fact, God often deprives us of things that would distract us from pursuing spiritual goals. He places higher value on character attainment, which will lead us into greater Christ-likeness, than on the comforts and superficial happiness that come with material prosperity. A very important part of modeling Christ is trusting God, which can be clearly seen if we follow the "fallow ground" principle.

Remission and Liberation in the King's Community

Remission of debts and liberation of slaves were closely linked practices because of the ancient way of handling indebtedness. When one person became indebted to another and was unable to pay, the debtor and his family could be taken as slaves or sold into slavery to repay the creditor. Purchasing freedom under such circumstances was nearly impossible. During Jubilee Year, however, indentured slaves were to be liberated. They no longer had to serve their creditors, nor were they obligated to pay off the previous debt. Although this may have seemed unfair to those who had loaned money in good faith, in the communal setting in which the Israelites first lived—and which would be duplicated in the early days of Christianity—the economic model was cooperation, not competition.

The kingdom of God is based on the character of God, and it is his nature to forgive. The Lord's Prayer expresses the importance of remission of debts in the statement, "Forgive us our debts, as we also have forgiven our debtors" (Matthew 6:12). The Greek verb for "forgive" means remit, which signifies erasing monetary debts in the most material sense possible. In reciting the Lord's Prayer, we often use "trespasses" in place of "debts." This is really not the best rendering, because "trespass" does not convey a financial meaning. In the Lord's Prayer, Jesus was not merely recommending that we should pardon those who have offended us; he was telling us that God will erase our indebtedness to him in proportion to our willingness to stop holding others under our power with our money. You can see that Jubilee living is central to this idea.

John Howard Yoder suggests that "the Our Father" is genuinely a "Jubilary Prayer." He goes on to note, "He who was not legalistic at any other point and who was ready without any hesitation to pardon prostitutes and disreputable people was nonetheless extremely strict upon one point: 'Only he who practices grace can receive grace.'"[16]

Jesus' parable of the unmerciful servant (Matthew 18:23-35) amplifies the importance of giving grace in order to receive grace. In the story, Jesus compares the kingdom of heaven to a certain king who decided to settle his accounts with his servants. One servant, owing several million dollars, begged not to be sold into slavery with his wife and children in spite of his obligation. The king felt compassion and remitted the man's indebtedness.

That servant, however, located a fellow worker who owed him just a small sum of money, and vehemently insisted that he pay the debt immediately. The debtor's plea for mercy was refused, and he was cast into prison until he could pay off what he owed. When other servants saw what had happened, they reported all this to their master, who summoned the wicked servant and said, "Shouldn't you have had mercy on your fellow servant just as I had on you?" The king was so moved with anger that he handed him over to the jailers to be tormented until he could pay all that he owed. Jesus summed up the parable by saying, "This is how my heavenly Father will treat each of you unless you forgive your brother from your heart" (Matthew 18:35).

The purpose for this Jubilee instruction was to illustrate the nature of kingdom community life to the people of God so they would understand that the welfare of other individuals was more important than higher economic status for themselves. Jubilee obedience would also resolve Israel's social problems by enabling its people to move ahead from poverty into normal living. Conversely, those who were financially fortunate would move back to a place of greater dependence on God and thus a better relationship with him. Jubilee living is central to life in the kingdom of God. Those who refuse to live with a Jubilee attitude and lifestyle are not welcome in the kingdom because they are rejecting its social and economic order.

Although our society does not punish indebtedness by enforced servitude, Jubilee principles have application today, though perhaps only in the church fellowship. We Christians are not instructed to overthrow the social and economic order of our nation. Nor are we called on to be advocates of a socialistic or communal economic system. While those who are honest about biblical interpretation realize that a sanctified socialism under the lordship of Jesus Christ is closer to the heart of the kingdom of God than competitive capitalism, we must recall that living in a fallen age as a fallen race makes every economic system less than utopian. The self-centeredness of man is always the determining factor in the failure of any social and economic order. Unqualified socialism assumes an overly optimistic view of the nature of man, as communist societies have illustrated, but competitive capitalism encourages the human tendency toward greed.

Redistribution of Capital

Although Jubilee principles cannot readily be applied to life in the secular world, should we not seek to apply them within the family of God? Churches need not become holy communes, and Christians need not join an order of poverty, but the church must illustrate the nature of the kingdom by encouraging Christians of financial means to take greater responsibility for those in their body who obviously suffer lack. This issue is difficult and sensitive because self-righteous almsgiving is too frequently the result. Nevertheless, only if the church develops greater caring for its own and also reaches out to the broader community will we enter into the heart of Jubilee living, which implies a more equitable distribution of God's bounty.

When the Jubilary concept was first introduced, most Jews earned their living off the land, which their herds and flocks grazed on, or was tilled and sowed for crops. Although the Israelites occupied the Promised Land as part of God's covenant with Abraham, they were never to be considered the actual owners of this land, but merely stewards or trustees. God would always be the owner and his people were to be guests on his property (Leviticus 25:23). Unfortunately, the Jews fell to the same wrong idea that we often hold when we assume that we have free and clear title to whatever we possess or occupy.

When God brought his people out of exile, each tribe and family was given part of the land to "own" and manage. As economic differences developed over the course of centuries, land was sold, bought, and traded. Some people became indebted and thus enslaved. Because the entire system periodically got out of balance, God required that every fifty years the land be returned to the original occupying families. Of course, this rule carried out literally would suggest some tempting possibilities to those who wanted to turn it to their economic advantage. Therefore, the Book of Leviticus contains some qualifications governing the redemption of property. God did not intend that the Jews would ever become economically competitive with each other. He was always eager for them to have a sense of care and responsibility for one another.

Kingdom Economics

In the days of Jesus, earning a living included far more variety than just agriculture. Jesus' own family lived by the carpentry trade, whereas some of his followers were fishermen. Nevertheless, the principle of divesting oneself of property entanglements was part of Jesus' call to discipleship. In our text in Luke 12, Jesus concluded by saying:

> *Do not be afraid, little flock, for your Father has been pleased to give you the kingdom. Sell your possessions and give to the poor. Provide purses for yourselves that will not wear out, a treasure that will not be exhausted, where no thief comes near and no moth destroys. For where your treasure is, there you heart will be also.* Luke 12:32-34

Few people today would doubt that this, indeed, is a radical saying. If taken literally by every Christian, the impact on the world's economy would be tumultuous, if not catastrophic. Christians would soon be a huge financial burden to the rest of society. On the other hand, we do an injustice to the concept of discipleship by relegating these verses strictly to the first century, or applying them today only to those who take a vow of poverty upon joining a religious order. What relevance do these verses have for modern societies?

Not all the disciples of Jesus abandoned their property and followed him on the dusty trails of Galilee and Judea. For example, a number of women willingly provided for the needs of Jesus and his followers. Mary and Martha, sisters of Lazarus, had a home in Bethany where Jesus occasionally stayed. The mother of John Mark owned a house in Jerusalem where the early Christian church met, probably including the upper room that was visited by the Holy Spirit during Pentecost. We, therefore, can conclude that even some of the closest friends of Jesus retained possession of their property. Probably these people were mentioned in Scripture precisely because they were generous in using their goods for the Lord's work.

> We are to understand that success in the kingdom of God is never measured by what we have, but by what we are becoming.

Because possession of property is a very personal issue, we put ourselves in spiritual danger when we prescribe rules by which we expect others to live. Nevertheless, Jesus calls us away from material independence and toward contentment. He expects us to abandon all preoccupations that cater to our self-sufficiency and entangle us in worldly concerns. We are to understand that success in the kingdom of God is never measured by what we have, but by what we are becoming. For most of us, modeling the kingdom qualities that God wants is more easily attained by owning less and living frugally than by striving for goods and temporal pleasures.

Discipleship Principle #11: Living Carefree

Jesus himself was a poor man according to worldly standards. He was born into abject poverty in a stable, spent most of his time with the poorer social class, and died possessing only the garments he wore. But imagine what he might have accrued during his days on earth! How much would Jairus, the synagogue official, have been willing to pay for his daughter to be brought back to life? How much could Jesus have charged the centurion for healing his servant? How much could Jesus have charged the hungry people for the multiplied loaves and fish? How often could he have sent Peter to the sea to pull up a fish with a coin in its mouth or filled his nets with fish? How much could he have charged the ten lepers for healing them?

Such questions could go on and on, citing all the ways Jesus ministered sensationally to others. But Jesus never cashed in on his power. In fact, he taught that poverty is a blessing when it enriches our spirituality. We know that Jesus did not proclaim Jubilee Year for kingdom living merely to abolish poverty by redistributing tangible goods. Rather, Jesus wanted others to see the principles of God's kingdom expressed by his followers. Disciples are honorable, contented people who know how to forgive debts and live carefree, trusting in God's provisions. They do not use money as an instrument of power, because they understand that all material resources belong to a loving God who has sovereignty regarding their distribution. Being liberated from our own materialistic concerns allows us to concentrate on the well-being of others, which is the point of Discipleship Principle #11:

Discipleship Principle #11
Sabbath and Jubilee principles, with their economic, social, and theological implications, must govern a disciple's everyday lifestyle.

PART THREE:

Learning Kingdom Leadership

Chapter 12

MANAGING WISELY: TRUSTWORTHINESS

Luke 16:1-13

Discipleship Principle #12
Disciples of the kingdom practice spiritual shrewdness, which reflects the faithful and wise stewardship of all resources, especially human relationships.

M ost followers of Christ learn quite early that they must walk the tightrope of living in the culture(s) of this world and the culture of the kingdom of God. It is an ongoing tension—very easy to fall off the rope onto either side. Achieving the balance of being "in the world, but not of it" is one of the disciples' most important lessons. Although some believers do, indeed, need to hear a strong admonition to put to death their worldly ways, others must be encouraged to see that discipleship does not require severance of all worldly connections. One can be God's *good and faithful servant* (Matthew 25:21) in a world that is hostile to kingdom standards.

Early in my ministry as a youth pastor, this issue threatened to explode our entire youth program. Some of the teenagers were from homes where the parents were new Christians, still learning how to respond obediently to Scripture and not yet exposed to the many extra-biblical scruples of evangelical/ fundamental Christians. These new believers continued to have active relationships with unbelievers, many of whom they were trying to win for Christ. Similarly, their teenagers were socially involved with two groups of friends: those at school and those at church.

Some long-time members of the congregation criticized the teenagers of the newer Christians. Shouldn't they stop going to school parties? Shouldn't they escape the "evil influences" of their non-Christian friends? In fact, shouldn't they attend a Christian high school?

Polarization was beginning to occur, and because I was reluctant to encourage arbitrary standards of spirituality, my own reputation was in jeopardy. In our church was a mature Christian couple whom I deeply respected; they were neither judgmental nor intolerant. Their own teenagers were somehow able to walk the tightrope, having close friends at school and also maintaining their Christian standards in a faithful but non-combative manner. Needing some encouragement, under the guise of a pastoral visit I broached the subject to the parents one day, asking what had been their strategy. Their answer was simple and profound, easily memorable, and frequently useful: "It is our policy to insulate our kids, not isolate them." The concept clicked immediately, but they went on to explain how it worked.

Isolating ourselves from the world means withdrawing and escaping as much of its influence as possible, including people whose values are different from our own. But this is not the kind of separation prescribed by Scripture. Jesus prayed, "...not that you take them out of the world but that you protect them from the evil one" (John 17:15). The opposite of being isolated from the world is being *immersed* in it. And, of course, that's not right either. Being *insulated,* however, allows us to be *in* the world but not *of* it, for we are then protected while we are there—the ideal way for a Christian to live. Being insulated does not exempt us from criticism, temptation, or occasional failure, but it does provide the opportunities to succeed as disciples. On the other hand, isolating ourselves from the world guarantees failure. Our separation is to be from sin and unto God, not from sinners and unto self-righteousness.

Comfortable with Sinners

The text for this chapter, Luke 16:1-13, is the fourth of five parables strung together. While the disciples were present to hear all five, only of the fourth one does the text specifically say that Jesus "told his disciples." (The other four seem to have been addressed to the Pharisees.) The first three parables are about the lost sheep, the lost coin, and the lost son (prodigal son). Jesus affirmed in all three of them the value of the lost item and the owner's urgent efforts to recover it. The shepherd would leave the ninety-nine sheep to look for the lost one; the woman would exhaust herself until she found the lost coin; the father of the prodigal son would not give up hope that his rebellious son would return, and he was ready to forgive and restore him to the family.

These three wonderful stories, which express so beautifully God's merciful love, follow an amazing verse that gives us important insight into the character of Jesus: "Now the tax collectors and 'sinners' were all gathering around to hear him" (Luke 15:1). When Christians talk about their desire to be "more Christ-like," they are most often referring to his godly character and conduct. But one of the features of Jesus that sometimes escapes our notice is that not only was he comfortable being with sinners, but—more remarkably—*they* were comfortable with him and actually enjoyed his company. Perhaps the significance of this is not immediately apparent. Bring it into the twenty-first century, and consider how many religious leaders and other righteous people freely mix with non-Christians *because* the *non-Christians enjoy their company.* I have been privileged to know a few great Christians like that. One of them was the senior pastor of the church mentioned above, where I was youth pastor and where there were so many new Christians. I suspect there is a relationship between his winsome spirit and the many who came to Christ under his ministry.

The obvious message Jesus was sending the Pharisees through the parables was that just as the sheep, coin, and son were very valuable and worth recovering at great sacrifice, so were the tax collectors and other sinners. But recovering them would demand personal involvement and compassion, not detachment and criticism.

Jesus then turned from the Pharisees, tax collectors, and sinners to tell his disciples a parable. (The Greek text uses a special construction at the beginning of Luke 16 to emphasize that Jesus deliberately turned to the disciples to deliver this parable to them.) What was his special message to them at this time, and what prompted it? Two ideas come to mind. One is found in the use of an uncommon word in both 15:13 and 16:1. The prodigal son *squandered* his wealth, and the shrewd manager had been accused of *wasting* his master's possessions. The two English words are translations of the same Greek word. The use of this rare word in referring to financial irresponsibility provides one clue as to why Jesus told this parable to the disciples. We should also note that the theme of the parable was already being exemplified in Jesus' acceptance by "sinners." Fostering profitable relationships is not only shrewd, but also good stewardship. Because this parable is complex and confusing, we must examine its elements before pondering its message.

The Clever Rascal

We must first understand that Jesus used different kinds of teaching illustrations. Not all of them were spoken parables. For example, mingling freely with sinners was one of his most powerful moral lessons. The scholar Joachim Jeremias points out that the Last Supper was a parabolic act, as were the feet washing, the temple cleansing, and the fig-tree cursing. William Barclay speaks of parables that work by analogy, parables of character study, and parables of contrast.[17] There are only three that fit into this last category, including the one before us. The other two are in Luke 11:5-8 and 18:1-8. Of Luke 16:1-13, Barclay says, "This parable is unique in that every character in it is a rascal."[18] T.W. Manson calls it the parable of the "clever rascal."

The story contains several contrasts: the unethical strategy of the manager versus the integrity that disciples must maintain; being welcomed into temporal houses versus admission to eternal dwellings; worldly wealth versus true riches; devotion to money versus devotion to God; and trustworthiness versus dishonesty.

Before looking for the main lesson, let's be sure we understand the content. Because the manager had been either dishonest or ineffective as a financial steward of the owner's estate, he was being fired. Not wanting to work a manual job or beg, he devised a plan intended to endear himself to his business clients, people who were indebted to his boss. Calling them together, he gave them each the opportunity to alter their account statements to their own advantage. This, of course, was meant to win their favor and therefore make them more likely to help him after his termination. The owner of the estate was impressed with his manager's shrewdness. While it appears that by lowering the payback the steward was being unethical in stealing part of the profit from the owner, that may not have been the case. Often a manager would agree to farm the property of an owner for a fixed fee. Whatever extra profit he could earn was his payment. In essence, he was a share-cropper. Thus, it is likely that the steward was forfeiting his own income, not that of the owner. This explanation helps us understand why the owner approved the steward's shrewdness.

Jesus' concern — seen by the approval of the owner — is best described by the phrase "stewardship of relationships." People of the world, although operating within a self-serving ethical framework, are so shrewd that the people of God can learn a lesson from them. In other words, within our kingdom community we should do all we can to keep good relationships with everyone, using our resources to bless others. Some of those tax collectors and other sinners gathered around Jesus might be the very friends the disciples would someday need. No doubt the work of Jesus and his followers during those three years was even then being financed by people whose lives they had blessed—probably people the Pharisees would scorn. Unlike the Pharisees, the One who offers us eternity cares more about restoring lost people and redeeming relationships than he does about scruples and sanctimony.

Christian Savvy

The lesson of the parable, then, is that just as people of this world have the smarts to employ relationships to their own advantage, so should disciples of the kingdom have the savvy, or spiritual shrewdness, to foster relationships that will accrue to the advantage of the eternal world. From this parable and the succeeding verses, Jesus taught five principles about trustworthiness, the wise management of God's resources.

First, trustworthiness enables us to use all our relationships to further the kingdom of God (vv. 8-9). Many Christians, clergy in particular, pride themselves in being culturally detached or removed, assuming that the world has nothing to teach them. I remember as a young teenager learning how lacking in business sense one pastor seemed to be. He was a godly man, and I diligently took notes of his sermons because I admired his spiritual depth. But a fair amount of my respect evaporated one Saturday. He had a big Oldsmobile 98 that he asked me to "Simonize," assuring me of payment for my work. A wax job in those days cost about twenty dollars in an auto shop. Six hours later, after I had that machine glistening, Pastor Stevens inspected it, praised me highly for doing such a great job, and then handed me a dollar bill. Since I had decided not to take anything for the work anyway, I tried to decline his "generosity." He insisted, saying that the Scripture says, "The laborer is worthy of his hire." I went away with an aching body, a dollar bill, and a tarnished view of my pastor's common sense that made me glad his frugality had not been with a non-Christian.

Looking back, I realize that I was not disappointed as much by the token pay as by his naiveté. How could a man be so brilliant behind the pulpit on Sundays and be so out of step with the real world? Although I knew he was not being stingy or trying to cheat me, this new perception of my pastor bothered me. You might say we should not place any person on a pedestal, so this is a good lesson for me. Unfortunately, this characterization of clergy being out of step with real life is quite common—and it can limit their effectiveness in the secular world.

Because being worldly wise is not sinful, it follows that being naïve about the ways of business, finance, psychology, sociology, and modern technology is not intrinsically spiritual. To establish rapport with people who desperately need to know about the eternal world, we need to show an interest in them and learn about their present circumstances. Jesus told his followers to be "as shrewd as snakes and as innocent as doves" (Matthew 10:16). Many Christians are strong on the innocent but weak on the shrewd. Too often we Christians needlessly turn off unbelievers by our overblown piety. Even when we don't make enemies in the secular world because of our zeal for Christ, sometimes we are dismissed because of our social clumsiness and general lack of *savor faire*. I'm convinced that many Christians avoid cocktail parties and other "worldly" events not because of religious scruples as much as the fear of being embarrassed by their inexperience with social protocol and "small talk."

Can you imagine Jesus saying, "We'll never get these tax collectors and prostitutes to the synagogue, so, I guess we cannot reach them?" Being stewards of relationships means moving out of our comfort zones to mix freely with unbelievers. Being welcomed among sinners is not necessarily proof of spiritual maturity, but surely it is significant when it occurs *for Jesus' sake*. God's people should be alert and congenial, interested in their surroundings, and involved in human issues.

> Being stewards of relationships means moving out of our comfort zones to mix freely with unbelievers.

Second, Jesus taught that because spiritually shrewd people have integrity, they can be entrusted with much as well as with very little (v. 10). Trustworthiness will be consistent within an individual, and so will dishonesty. A trustworthy person cannot be bought at any price. Like Jesus, who refused "all the kingdoms of the world and their splendor" when tempted by the devil (Matthew 4:8-10), a trustworthy disciple sees that no earthly treasure can compare with the promise of eternal glory.

Trustworthiness is one of the most admirable of human qualities. It encompasses such other attributes as honesty, benevolence, confidentiality, loyalty, and dependability. People who embody these characteristics will always be given responsibility. People with high intelligence, compelling charisma, and powerful influence often fail in leadership positions because they are deficient in trustworthiness. Although they talk a good job and are usually able to excuse their failures convincingly, their efforts will end in shame. Like King Saul, who outwardly was the pride of Israel, at some point they break trust and ruin themselves and those depending upon them. Far better to have a leader like David who, although he stumbled morally several times, remained worthy of the trust that his subjects and God had placed in him.

The third lesson in this parable is that trustworthiness with things of this world qualifies us to be entrusted with "true riches" (v. 11), which are qualitatively different from anything in the world. Most likely Jesus was referring here to spiritual treasure, the human soul. Spiritual responsibility should never be given to those who have not previously proven themselves trustworthy with material possessions. Only people who manage worldly resources faithfully can handle responsibility for the care of souls.

Never have I had a more avid, capable assistant than Andrew, who had overcome a serious chemical addiction. He was tireless and talented. He worked well with people, and was so eager to learn. No job seemed too big or too small for him to tackle. For months we worked well together, until...; until my treasurer brought to my attention some unexpected credit card bills. The long and short of it was that Andrew had found ways of stealing thousands of dollars from the church and "borrowing" hundreds from people who trusted him. We tried in many ways over many months to restore him, but he was addicted to deception. While he needed the money because he was a bad steward of his finances, I think he was even more attracted to his life of subterfuge because of the pride of being able to pull it off. Sadly, to this day, he has not recovered.

Besides Jesus Christ, the person in Scripture who probably best exemplified trustworthiness was Joseph, favored son of the Old Testament patriarch Jacob. Sold into slavery in Egypt, he earned such high respect that Pharaoh placed into his hands the fate of the entire nation during a time of famine. Joseph's story is particularly apt here because although technically only Egypt's future was in his administrative hands, much more than that was at stake. God was using Joseph's trustworthiness with the food supply of the Egyptians to ensure the future of Israel, and thus the redemptive purpose to be accomplished in Christ. Joseph may not have realized he was the guardian of "true riches," but that did not matter. His faithfulness with Egypt's material wealth qualified him to be entrusted with God's greater riches.

Fourth, while we are only stewards of worldly wealth, that stewardship is also a spiritual responsibility (v. 12). We are merely managers, not owners, of all we have. Many other parables and teachings of Jesus reveal this. God owns the world he has created, and how we manage those resources reveals whether we are competitors with God or submissive to his will. Although God does not begrudge us his property, he is jealous about his sovereignty. Because he is also concerned for our well-being, we are warned not to try to serve two masters (v. 13). The tithe, which God required of the Israelites, was meant to be a tangible reminder of God's ownership of the fields, crops, and livestock. Our giving certainly ought to demonstrate the same spirit, and the best proof of that attitude is our giving unto the Lord first—before paying bills or indulging our desires. The rule for Israel was "the first and the best." When we only give God the convenient or the leftovers, our shallow understanding is obvious and insulting to God. Some people assume that God is not interested in money and materials, forgetting that he made it all. In reality, money is a sacred trust and needs to be treated sacramentally. Being godly managers of material goods is a high spiritual responsibility. The reverence a Roman Catholic priest shows for the crumbs of the Communion host is symbolic of the way we all should care for the gifts God entrusts to us.

Fifth, Jesus taught that it is futile to try to be a servant of the kingdom if we are devoted to feathering our own nest (v. 13). We cannot serve two masters. If we try to serve "Money" (capitalized as if it were the name of a god), we "despise" God. Strong language, but this is an important issue. No wonder "the Pharisees, who loved money, heard all this and were sneering at Jesus" (v. 14).

Illustration of this parable appears in the next one, the rich man and Lazarus (Luke 16:19-31). The rich man, tormented in Hades, begged for help from Lazarus, who formerly begged at the rich man's gate and ate his crumbs but was now comfortably situated with Abraham. The implication is that the rich man failed to use his worldly wealth to win friendship with someone who could welcome him into an eternal dwelling place. In other words, the rich man was not "spiritually shrewd" in his relationship with Lazarus.

Life's Ledger

Spiritual shrewdness — trustworthiness — is a quality we must exercise if we are to make wise investments of our total resources. Imagine for a moment that you are a corporation, and all the investments of your life are quantified on a ledger. God, the only stockholder, wants to analyze cost efficiency to determine the profitability of You, Inc. Suppose this occurs near the end of your time on earth—say, age 82. God has given you almost 30,000 days to use his world and entrusted you with X number of abilities and X number of opportunities. If your average annual income over forty years was $50,000, for 40 years of work, you have received about $2,000,000 for material resources. God has blessed you by providing immediate access, help when needed, and a very generous package of perks. As owner, God has every right to expect a good return on his investment. Now he is ready to analyze whether your corporation has been profitable. He has created you, made provision to save you, and stood by to help in every worthwhile venture you wanted to undertake. What does the bottom line on your life's ledger reveal?

This is a rather crass way of looking at our relationship to God, for we are family to him, not part of a portfolio. However, the analogy does point out the truth that we are not sovereign owners of any aspects of our lives. The parable of the talents in Matthew 25:14-30 has a similar message. God has entrusted each of us with varying amounts of "talents" in the form of financial resources, spiritual gifts, opportunities, relationships, and experiences. His purpose will not be accomplished if we cautiously bury this wealth. He expects us to be shrewd investors, and he will look for a generous return. The issue here is not how many resources he has entrusted to each of us, but how we use whatever we have been given. (The parable of the talents would have made the same point if the servant with five talents had buried his and the servant with only one had invested wisely.) Jesus commended a poor widow for giving "two very small copper coins" to the temple treasury (Luke 21: 1-4). Because she gave out of her poverty, she had given more than all the others, who gave out of their wealth.

The critical question here is, "What determines how I invest my life?" In talking with many people about this issue, I have come to believe that the answer is always the same: Our view of reality determines how we invest. Jesus said that "where your treasure is, there your heart will be also" (Matthew 6:21). Our investments are a sure indication of what we believe to be most important. It is not the other way around. The text does not say that we invest where our heart is; that would be great. Unfortunately, our heart follows our investments. If we want our heart to seek first God's kingdom, then our finances and other resources need to go there first.

To expose your view of reality, you might want to answer several other questions:

1. What is your everyday, out-in-the-world view of God? Do you really believe a Supreme Being exists? If so, what is he like? Is he involved? Is he personal? How "big" is he? Are you accountable to God?

2. What is your view of time? Is time the only dimension of existence? Or is there eternity? Who owns time? Are you free to use time as you wish?

3. What is your view of humanity? Are we temporary or eternal beings? Are we permanently lost or redeemable? Are we programmed or responsible? What determines our destiny?

4. What is your view of Jesus Christ? Is he alive or dead? Is he God? How does he relate to today's world? What are his goals? Does he really want us to help him? If so, how?

5. What is your view of the church? Is it only a man-made institution or is it the community of God's people? Must you be involved with it? What are your responsibilities to the church? What are your responsibilities to people outside the fellowship of believers?

Answering questions like these may not be easy, but we answer them every day. We can't avoid it. Those committed to worldly values have the least difficult time with these questions. A blatant materialist, who believes that the world is just the product of space plus time plus chance (which is also a type of faith), may easily live consistently with his presupposition. In fact, consistency is not even an issue if there is no accountability. But the believer in God has a moral consciousness that makes these questions important. And if our investments are not consistent with our convictions, we will experience inner condemnation and tension. Part of the process of growing up spiritually is bringing our commitments into line with our faith. One pastor said it this way, "Seems like the last part of a man to get converted is his wallet." We are talking about more than just the contents of a wallet, but it is an apt symbol for our investments.

In/Of—Neither/Nor

Before leaving the topic of wise management, we should return to the stewardship of relationships. Living in two worlds that have conflicting standards is a way we share in Christ's sufferings. It is why we groan with the creation as we await our adoption as sons and daughters of God in the final redemption of the world. It is why we passionately pray, "Thy kingdom come." In his two-natured personhood, Jesus embodied this tension. To the extent that we try to be faithful to him, we live with the stress of furthering kingdom goals in a hostile environment.

A popular Christian cliché describes this paradox as being "in the world but not of it." A friend who reviewed the material for this book turned this saying inside-out and upside-down to explore the various alternatives. We Christians might live:

In but not of the world
Of but not in the world
Neither in nor of the world
In and of the world

Of-ness should be understood as referring to the source of our values—or to who/what owns us (who/what we are "of"). Clearly, many of our values—what shapes our decisions and our lives—all too frequently are the values "of" the world.

In-ness is the most difficult term. It refers to the practical notion of being significantly involved in the lives of others, making a worthwhile impact on them. In-ness is not merely a matter of associating with the world, being "nice" as we go through our daily routines. It requires involvement, going beyond superficiality when we relate to non-Christians. Too many Christians hold themselves apart from unbelievers for fear of being contaminated. Or for fear that it will get messy. This is a very unfortunate misunderstanding of being "not of the world."

Being *not of* the world refers to our affections and our values, not our daily involvements. In every circumstance our motives can be righteous. A Christ-like disciple should be able to maintain the integrity of his walk with God in even the most sinful environment on earth. This is not to suggest that we ought to put ourselves in temptation's path, but to assure us that finding ourselves in an ungodly atmosphere, does not mean we are "of" the world.

Most tragic is how easily we can view *not in* as a sign of spiritual purity and yet, in fact, be totally *of* the world, because we endorse its values. This is blatant hypocrisy, the kind Jesus severely condemned.

In our permissive society, the only critics of being *in* the world are super-conservative Christians. Others will not judge us for secular involvement, but for Jesus to be so involved with sinners was a lot more threatening to the establishment. Many of the Jews were scrupulous in their pietism. Nevertheless, Jesus repeatedly defiled their strict code by having close contact with many "unclean" elements of society. The extent of this courageous stand is shown in chapters 8 and 9 of Matthew's Gospel. Jesus became ceremoniously "defiled" by his contact with each of the following:

- A leper (8:1-4)
- A Gentile soldier (8:5-13)
- Many demonized people (8:16-17)
- The sea (8:23-27)
- Tombs, demoniacs, and swine (8:28-32)
- A paralyzed sinner (9:1-6)
- Sinners and a tax collector (9:9-13)
- A woman with menstrual hemorrhaging (9:20-22)
- A corpse (9:23-25)
- More demons (9:32-34)
- All kinds of diseases and sickness (9:35-36)

Jesus was not a very holy person by the standards of his day! But sometimes it takes getting dirty to deal with the dirt. Jesus had, and still has, the amazing ability to love sinners yet hate sin. For many Christians today, however, keeping sin and sinners lumped together and shunning both is more respectable and convenient. They mistakenly think this is the only way to stay clean.

Discipleship Principle #12: Managing Wisely

Assessing the four options discussed above, being in and of the world is shamelessly sinful; being neither in nor of the world is pseudo-spiritual; being of but not in the world is hypocrit-ical—but being in but not of the world is true Christ-likeness. Only those who are *in,* really in, but *not of* the world are disciples whom Christ can trust with the spiritual responsibility to be his ambassadors of reconciliation in this alien and hostile world. They are wise managers who are trustworthy in both little and much and therefore practice Discipleship Principle #12.

Discipleship Principle #12
Disciples of the kingdom practice spiritual shrewdness, which reflects the faithful and wise stewardship of all resources, especially human relationships.

Chapter 13

CONFRONTING SIN: ACCOUNTABILITY

Luke 17:1-10

Discipleship Principle # 13
Disciples must become accountable, which entails confronting sin in each other courageously and compassionately, for the purpose of stimulating each other's spiritual advancement.

The Bible has much to say about accountability. Luke 17:1 is a good place to start because there the Greek word *skandala* appears. Notice that this was another occasion when Jesus addressed his remarks directly to his disciples, so we have in these verses another discipleship teaching passage. In the New International Version, *skandala* is translated "things that cause people to sin." Other translations say "stumbling blocks" or "things that make people fall," since *skandala* was the word for a root growing out of the ground on a path, or a protruding rock too massive to be unearthed.

Apart from the occasional camping or hunting trip, most of us today do not walk on dirt trails, although this was commonplace in Jesus' day. Protruding roots or rocks threatened every step.

They can trip you up, even injure you, just as sin can do. Perhaps this is the same imagery Paul had in mind when he warned, "Be careful how you walk" (Ephesians 5:15 NASB).

Not long ago I went to a camping site to pick up my son after a week of church camp. After dinner, all the campers were excited about the talent show they would perform for the parents near the campfire, which was about a half-mile away from the main complex. Walking along the wooded pathway in the dark proved to be a challenge not relished by most of the adults. The designated "torchbearers" (flashlight carriers) were not overly sympathetic with the adults' relatively slow pace and were prone to run ahead. It was quite obvious how utterly dependent we were upon the torchbearers, and this became for me an apt illustration of the critical need for accountability. As long as the torchbearers and adults stayed in right relation to each other, the *skandala* were not a threat. When the light ran ahead or we lagged behind it, toes were stubbed on roots or rocks and people began tripping. Being in the light and close to the people bearing the light became very important to us. And so it is in the Christian life. The same idea and words are used in 1 John 2:10, "Whoever loves his brother lives in the light, and there is nothing in him to make him stumble."

A Tree in the Sea

Jesus' teaching in the text we are considering is thought by many to be a series of four unrelated but linked ideas:

Verses 1-2	Warning about causing others to sin
Verses 3-4	Command to be forgiving
Verses 5-6	Statement about faith
Verses 7-10	Parable about duty (a servant's role)

The connection between them is not easily made, but I believe it can be demonstrated that the four sections made up one teaching given by our Lord to his disciples. The key to seeing the links is in the concepts of roots (*skandala*, v.1, and "uprooted," v.6) and "the sea" (vv. 2 and 6). Thematically, the passage is in a section of Luke's Gospel (chapters 15-17) in which Jesus was contrasting for his followers the ways and teaching of the Pharisees with his own expectations and thoughts on those subjects. He was also warning his disciples that the Pharisees would be a source of trouble for them, and most likely that is what he had in mind in Luke 17:1-2. The "little ones" whom the Pharisees would mislead were his followers, insignificant people in the social economy of Judea. Jesus then warned his disciples to "watch yourselves," or be on guard for each other. That phrase in verse 3 is more literally translated, "Constantly be looking out for one another." Like the Pharisees, the disciples would find themselves offending and even sinning against each other. They would need to be courageous in confronting the sin and quick in forgiving each other an unlimited number of times.

Because the disciples thought such an expectation was beyond them, they asked Jesus to give them more faith (v.5). His reply takes us back to the imagery of the roots and the sea. Whereas he has already told them that the one who was a stumbling block would be better off having been thrown into the sea with a millstone around his neck (v.2), he now tells them that with a small but growing faith they can uproot the whole tree, stumbling roots and all, and have it thrown into the sea. In other words, if the disciples operate together on the basis of faith, the *skandala* themselves, which are the sins that come between brothers, will be eliminated. Faith is the binding force that both brothers—the offender and the rebuker—have in common, and it enables them to stay in a brotherly relation despite offenses and rebuking.

A loose paraphrase of the ideas in the first six verses may help. Jesus was telling his disciples that religious leaders might lead people into sin, causing them to stumble over spiritual roots on the paths they would tread. Those who cause this stumbling would be better off being thrown into the sea. Because even the disciples, as future spiritual leaders, would sin against each other, they had better learn to rebuke, repent, and forgive. Being unsure of their ability to do this, the disciples asked Jesus to increase their faith, to which he replied that with even a little faith on the part of both the offender/repenter and the rebuke/forgiver, the roots of offense and the entire "mulberry tree" (known for its elaborate root system) *rather than the offender*, would be cast into the sea. Rebuking, repenting, and forgiving an offence separates the sin from the sinner and enables God to judge the sin and spare the sinner, who is thus able to return to fellowship with the brother he had offended.

As difficult as this expectation may have seemed, Jesus reinforced it by telling the short parable in verses 7-10. The servant (or "slave" in some translations) who had been working hard all day would still be expected to perform his duties as a servant when he returned to the master. Just as it was not unreasonable to expect him to continue obeying, it was not unreasonable to expect the disciples to continue to be faithful to the Lord's command to hold each other accountable and be forgiving.

The Ministry of Rebuking

Jesus knew that the human tendency to undermine the spiritual standards of others existed even in his followers, so he gave them a very serious warning about the consequences of inhibiting others from making spiritual progress. Christian disciples enjoy great liberty, especially when compared to the legalistic Pharisees, but such freedom can easily develop into a license in ethical standards that may be especially harmful to less mature believers. The liberty that Jesus modeled for his followers must be used prudently, which is why he told them to "watch" themselves.

In the 1980s the evangelical church in America was suddenly hit by repeated scandals involving Christian celebrities.

All the drama normally associated with afternoon soap operas could be seen on the nightly news as several famous Christians "fell" to financial fraud, adultery, pornography, and assorted other sins. The church, which had enjoyed "the Decade of the Evangelicals," was now being ridiculed by the world. It was like finding a Puritan in a brothel. In shame, we Christians found ourselves awkwardly explaining to the general public that each scandal was a rare exception. But then another one would hit the headlines. To avoid embarrassment, some believers stopped witnessing. Others stopped giving to Christian ministries.

A very fundamental Christian dynamic had been neglected by these fallen leaders: *accountability*. No doubt each one agreed with the theological concept of unity in the body of Christ, which presupposes accountability, but the theology was not translated into life. In fact, one well-known Christian leader, who repented after stumbling into sin, reported in a Christian magazine that the hectic pace of his ministry caused him to abandon relationships of accountability—the main reason for his fall. Many excuses could be offered for this omission: celebrity status (which makes it difficult for a leader to remain in close fellowship with his flock); the temptations that accompany frequent travel; the "electronic church" (which can too easily separate a Christian leader from a caring congregation); and the sense that one's mission is so essential that some indiscretions pale to insignificance. There are a host of other rationalizations, but more basic than any of them—and a plague to the modern church—is an unbiblical phenomenon highly admired in our day: rampant individualism. It is one of the worst "isms" around—dare we call it the unknown god in our society? Individualism often translates into isolation, which makes accountability difficult.

Perhaps the only effective way of watching ourselves is to be accountable to one another. This is exactly what Jesus taught when he exhorted his followers to exercise the ministry of rebuking brothers who sin. The verb for "rebuke" is found frequently in the New Testament. It means to express disapproval without threat of a particular punishment, to "censure." Often in Scripture a nonhuman force such as a demon, a fever, or the wind is rebuked (Luke 4:35, 39; 8:24), but rebukes from one person to another were usually disapproved by Jesus, as occurred when the disciples rebuked those who brought children to be blessed by Jesus (Matt. 19:13). In Mark 8:32 we see Peter rebuking Jesus for talking about his impending death. Of course, Jesus rebuked the rebuke. Peter's rebuke was inappropriate because it was based on his misunderstanding of Jesus' messianic mission. In fact, only once in the New Testament did Jesus allow an individual's spontaneous rebuke to pass unchallenged. This occurred on Golgotha, when one dying there rebuked the other for selfishly exploiting Christ's crucifixion (Luke 23:40).

The New Testament provides for only one kind of situation where a formal rebuke is allowable: the brotherly correction of another brother who is either sinning or causing others to sin. It is mentioned in the Luke 17 passage we are studying, and this teaching was also given by the Lord as the first part of the disciplinary function of the church (Matthew 18:15). Paul later mentioned this ministry more specifically to Timothy, whose pastoral duty was to "correct, rebuke and encourage—with great patience and careful instruction" (2 Timothy 4:2).

Rebuking is not commonly practiced in Christian circles today, at least not with a ministerial intent. Some are quite will practiced in the activity of rebuking, but not with the right motivation. When rebuking is done to discredit, embarrass, get even with, put down, humiliate, or hurt another person in any way, it is not biblical rebuking and cannot be considered part of discipleship. Rebuking another believer must always be done to restore and build up the offender. It is never proper to condemn the offender or to broadcast his failings to a larger audience so as to shame him.

The Christian and the Questionable

Sometimes honest differences of opinion arise regarding an activity. One person may take a freedom that another condemns simply because the two may have very different cultural and social backgrounds but find themselves in the same church. The one with certain scruples may with the best of intentions want to impose his standards on the other. Often in the church we assume that the person who lives by the most

> Often in the church we assume that the person who lives by the most "Don'ts" is the more mature, but that is not always the case.

"Don'ts" is the more mature, but that is not always the case. Who should be accountable to whom, and how are we to know whose standards are right?

Such questions surfaced not long into the early church's life. For example, some of the Christians in Corinth were guilty of abusing their liberty, and chapters 8-10 of Paul's first letter to the Corinthians address this issue. The specific activity being discussed was eating meat that had previously been used in pagan temples as gifts to so-called gods. The more enlightened Christians knew that such meat was no different materially from other meat, and treating it as different gave credibility to the superstitions of the false religion. Hence, these believers freely purchased and consumed the meat. Others, because of their cultural background, had greater sensitivity to idolatry and thus more scruples. For them, any association with pagan cults was idolatrous and possibly demonic.

Paul's teaching may surprise the new Bible student. We might think that Paul would side with the first group because of his great maturity and understanding. If the decision were to be made on knowledge alone, Paul surely would have agreed that the idols and religion they represented were meaningless and harmless to the Christian. Ethical decisions, however, should not be made on the basis of knowledge alone. Paul gave three reasons: knowledge tends to "puff up" (1 Corinthians 8:1); knowledge cannot free a person from a weak conscience (v. 7); and acting solely on knowledge may bring ruin to another whose conscience is thereby violated (vv. 11-12).

So what is to be the basis for making ethical decisions? When possible we should use the Bible, but the Bible does not address every issue specifically. It gives principles that need to be known and applied to situations for which Scripture does not give a hard-and-fast rule. The positive guidelines that Paul gave to the Corinthians may be applied to many questions of morality today. First, he told them to avoid the extreme—they should not go to pagan temples and eat meat, even for the sake of being neighborly with non-Christians (1 Corinthians 10:20-21). Certain places and activities have associations that compromise our loyalty, in the eyes of even the non-believing observer.

Second, Paul told them not to be overly scrupulous—they were to buy meat in the market without asking where it came from (1 Corinthians 10:26). The meat itself was not important, and they were not to make an issue out of it. Third, they were to exercise great caution and sensitivity when eating in an unbeliever's house. If nothing was said about the meat, they were free to enjoy it. If, however, someone mentioned that the meat had been offered as a sacrifice, a disciple was not to eat it, regardless of his own conscience (10:27-28). The person mentioning the sacrifice of the meat undoubtedly did so because he suspected such meat would not be appropriate for a Christian. All three principles demand that the disciple of Christ be accountable not only to specific Bible-based rules and his or her own conscience, but also to the rest of the body of Christ.

The Rewards of Accountability

I hope you are convinced about the importance of account-ability and its role in confronting sin. But what is its intrinsic value? Ideally, we will enter into relationships of accountability not only out of obedience to Christ's teachings but also because we have the added incentive of knowing it is to our advantage to do so. Personal gain may not be the noblest of reasons to comply, but it is certainly an effective motivator. Therefore, we need to see that accountability is rewarding—that it will increase our spiritual maturity and make us more effective disciples. Accountability may make us somewhat uncomfortable at first, but as we begin to experience its benefits, our motives will become purer and less self-serving.

What are some incentives that might encourage you to pursue accountability within the church fellowship? The primary payoff is the intrinsic value of such a relationship. Having a spiritual mentor is a key to effective accountability, and it is a very enriching experience. The disciples enjoyed following Jesus, not because they relished the tough demands he placed on them, but because they valued the time they spent with him. Someone has said that we know we love someone when we feel better about ourselves whenever we are with that person. So it was with Jesus' followers, and that is an important reward of spiritual mentoring. Being under the watchful, concerned care of a disciple-maker is a very affirming experience. Those who have had such a relationship speak of it as a time of peak fulfillment and growth in their life.

Another personal benefit from being in an accountability relationship is that all areas of your life are enhanced. For instance, if one of the disciplines you maintain is a daily time of private worship, and you also need to lose weight, you will be pleasantly surprised by the new resolve you will have in that endeavor as well. Quality of life improves greatly when someone else cares enough to keep checking on your progress and encouraging you toward your goals.

Accountability will also bring you new confidence in your ability to achieve. An undisciplined life is in disarray and invites defeat. While some people—a small minority—are self-motivated enough to enforce their own discipline, most of us need to be accountable to someone else to be successful. Once you taste success in an area that previously caused you frustration and anxiety, you will gain courage and believe that other successes are also possible. For example, many of us middle-aged and older folks have felt greatly threatened by the high-tech revolution of the past few decades. Computers can induce anxiety attacks in people whose jobs demand that they become computer literate! The claim that any computer hardware or software could be user-friendly seems misleading, if not an outright lie to such people. But being accountable to an employer's demands has motivated many otherwise reluctant people to join the computer set. Success breeds success, and accountability is the breeding ground.

Surely there are other incentives for entering an accountability relationship, but these three should be enough to get you started. Once you have taken the first step, you will need no more convincing.

Making Accountability Work

Although this book is not intended to be a how-to-manual, it may be helpful to suggest some practical ways to raise your accountability quotient. The first step is to choose an "accountant," someone to help keep track of your *spiritual* gains and shortfalls. This person may be a formal mentor to you or just a Christian friend. In fact, there are several possible arrangements that work. One-to-one peer accountability works for some. Here you agree with a Christian friend to be mutually accountable, with each of you taking responsibility for the other. Watch out, however, that this is not a blind-leading-the-blind situation (Luke 6:39).

An important ingredient in accountability is authority. If neither partner has authority, discipline may be hard to maintain. A one-on-one arrangement works best if one of the pair is considered the discipler or mentor. He or she should be someone whose life demonstrates both personal discipline and character maturity. Use the other kingdom qualities in this book to assess that maturity, and when you find a suitable mentor, submit to his or her spiritual authority. "But isn't that dangerous?" you might ask. Yes, it may be, but not as risky as not being accountable to anyone. A carefully selected mentor will rarely make unreasonable demands.

Better than a one-on-one arrangement, in my opinion, is small-group accountability. Its advantages are numerous. For one thing, it eliminates the risk of one person taking control. When four to eight people are involved in mutual accountability, the excesses of any one member will be offset by the others. Having access to different perspectives, gifts, personalities, and experiences also provides greater opportunities for the spiritual enrichment of each member. After working on discipleship as both a leader and a learner in many types of settings, I am convinced that growth is greater, better balanced, and more pleasant in the small-group experience. Certainly a leader should act as a moderator at the group meetings, but his or her job is to facilitate, not dominate. Again, the leadership role should be assigned to someone of sufficient spiritual maturity to achieve that purpose.

Biblical support for small-group accountability is found in the example of Jesus whose twelve disciples were subdivided into three groups for teaching purposes. John MacArthur, in his sermon series "The Master's Men,"[19] notes that every time the apostles are listed in the New Testament, four names are always grouped first, another four are grouped second, and a third four are listed last. Furthermore, each group may have had a designated group leader. Peter is always listed first in the first group, Philip is always listed first in the second group, and James the son of Alphaeus is always listed first in the third group. The order of names within the groupings changes from one passage to the next, but not the first name nor the order of the groups. It is highly possible that Jesus organized his men in small accountability groups for their own growth and to set a model for future generations of the church.

Although we lack the knowledge of exactly what went on in those groups, we can imagine the dynamics by understanding passages like the one before us in Luke 17. Here Jesus was telling his disciples to watch out for one another even to the point of rebuking each other for sin. The relationships were to be intensely honest and caring. But what specifically should occur in such a group?

The MasterWorks *Follow Me Group Guide* mentioned in the preface of this book provides discussion and activity opportunities that will enable a small group of Christians to stimulate each other toward vigorous spiritual growth. The basic goal is to further in every member the development of the kingdom qualities we have been examining. Discipleship is more a matter of growth in spiritual maturity than gaining personal disciplines or skills, as important as those things are. It is advisable to devote three or four weeks of attention to each character quality. Asking the right questions is the key to discovery, and the *Group Guide* consists mostly of probing questions that our experience has shown to be fruitful in encouraging growth.

Consider the way a skilled financial accountant works. He or she asks lots of questions, and the accuracy of the audit depends on whether the important questions are asked and answered properly. One discipleship organization suggests seventy-five questions that an aspiring disciple should discuss with the mentor. Unfortunately, most of them concern external behavior rather than character maturity, and some of them imply a rigid legalism that I cannot recommend. Nevertheless, the idea of using questions to discover growth opportunities, obstacles, and successes is excellent.

Jesus was highly skilled at asking questions. In fact, much of his teaching was given in answer to his own questions. In a sense, all of his questions had that rhetorical aspect, because Jesus did not need to ask questions to gain information. His questions were usually asked to provide spiritual insight and thereby stimulate growth. Look, for example, at some of the questions Jesus asked his followers in the discipleship passages of Luke:

- "If you love those who love you, what credit is that to you? ... And if you do good to those who are good to you, what credit is that to you? ... And if you lend to those from whom you expect repayment, what credit is that to you? ..." [6:32-34]
- "Can a blind man lead a blind man? Will they not both fall into a pit? ... Why do you look at the speck of sawdust in your brother's eye and pay no attention to the plank in your own eye? ... Why do you call me, 'Lord, Lord,' and do not do what I say?" [6:39, 41, 46]
- "Who do the crowds say I am? ... But what about you? ... Who do you say I am?" [9:18, 20]
- "Which of you fathers, if your son asks for a fish, will give him a snake instead? Or if he asks for an egg, will give him a scorpion? If you then, though you are evil, know how to give good gifts to your children, how much more will your Father in heaven give the Holy Spirit to those who ask him!" [11:11-13]
- "Who of you by worrying can add a single hour to his life? Since you cannot do this very little thing, why do you worry about the rest?" [12:25-26]
- "So if you have not been trustworthy in handling worldly wealth, who will trust you with true riches? And if you have not been trustworthy with someone else's property, who will give you property of your own?" [16:11-12]
- "For who is greater, the one who is at the table or the one who serves? Is it not the one who is at the table? ..." [22:27]

And so on. Admittedly, most of these are rhetorical questions, but their value lies in their ability to spur us along the road to spiritual maturity as we confront the sin in each other's lives.

One valuable tactic in small-group discipleship is to enter covenantal arrangements with one another. Set a time limit for your group involvement; you can always extend it, but without one, the group will lack discipline and purposefulness. Then declare to each other the areas of your life in which you know you need growth. You may feel that there are many areas, but choose one especially for the duration of the contract. Aim for character qualities rather than performance standards. The religious performance of the Pharisees was unparalleled, but that was not what God wanted.

> Aim for character qualities rather than performance standards. The religious performance of the Pharisees was unparalleled, but that was not what God wanted.

Perhaps you will choose "servanthood" as your quality for growth (see chapter 15). Although the group as a whole may focus on other aspects of discipleship much of the time—and you will grow in those areas—you will tenaciously pray about and give special attention to developing servanthood in your life. Others who are farther advanced in that quality will provide good examples and encouragement to you. Pay close attention to anyone who is gifted in serving others, observing both attitudes and actions. Ask that person to share insights that will help you and to pray particularly for you. When you have time to share with each other about your life during the previous week, reflect on the opportunities you had for serving others, and how you responded inwardly and outwardly to those opportunities. If you make sure the others in the group recognize your intense desire to gain a servant's spirit, they will make it part of their contract with you to stimulate your growth in that direction. You will be pleased to see that others in the group will in turn look to you for support in an area where you may be stronger than they are. This is exactly what it means to be accountable!

Discipleship Principle #13: Confronting Sin

Our Lord, the most self-sufficient person who has ever walked this earth, exemplified the kind of obedient humility that must underscore our efforts to achieve growth. Philippians 2:5 says, "Your attitude should be the same as that of Christ Jesus," and the next verses go on to describe how he laid aside his glory to take on humanity, humbling himself to learn and experience all that was God's will for him. Although verse four is often overlooked, it may summarize the idea hidden in the more familiar verses: "Each of you should look not only to your own interests, but also to the interests of others." That is, we must be accountable to other believers and on behalf of other believers, for this will ensure that we live according to Discipleship Principle #13:

Discipleship Principle # 13
Disciples must become accountable, which entails confronting sin in each other courageously and compassionately, for the purpose of stimulating each other's spiritual advancement.

Chapter 14

WORKING EXPECTANTLY: ALERTNESS

Luke 21:5-36

Discipleship Principle #14
Every day is lived and worked with a sense of anticipation and alertness by disciples because they expect that their Lord may return at any moment.

A s we near the end of the discipleship teaching passages in Luke's Gospel, we may be tempted to look back, review, evaluate, and revel in how far we have come. The theme of this next passage, however, will not allow us to do that, for it looks forward, not backward. Failing to be alert to what lies ahead causes us to hesitate in our mission. This proved to be the downfall of many Bible characters, most notably Lot's wife (Genesis 19:26) and all but a handful of Gideon's army (Judges 7: 3-8). Jesus knew that after he departed, the disciples would tend to reminisce about the good old days, but that would be disastrous because of what lay ahead. He knew his followers would need still another kingdom quality, so he seized the moment to teach them about alertness.

Most great people live expectantly, with vision and hope for the future. The nineteenth-century preacher Charles Spurgeon was such a man, and he taught others the same sense of optimistic anticipation. One day a young pastor who rarely had seen anyone converted through his ministry visited Spurgeon, and with great discouragement poured out his heart, hoping for either solace or advice. Instead, Spurgeon asked, "Well, what do you expect? Do you think that every time you preach a sermon someone will be converted?" The young man replied, "No, of course not." "That is precisely your problem," said Spurgeon. "What fisherman would ever throw in his hook and bait if he did not expect to catch something!"

Disciples of the kingdom are forward-looking people. We live expectantly, believing that the future belongs to Jesus because he is coming back to possess it and all that his Father created. But there is more ahead than his return. The Bible frequently speaks about the end times. All three synoptic Gospels record Jesus' "Apocalyptic Discourse" (Matthew 24, Mark 13, and Luke 21). Perhaps the most famous of all prophetic writings is the last book of the Bible. Its real title is "Apocalypse," from the Greek word meaning "revelation." This kind of writing, a distinct genre of literature that was popular during the two centuries before and two centuries after the birth of Jesus, contains many images and visions: word pictures used to depict dramatic events. The theme of apocalyptic writing is usually focused on the end times or some future catastrophic event. Although the imagery once had cultural relevance, twenty centuries later we find difficulty in understanding specific allusions recorded by John, the author, which is one reason why interpreting the Book of Revelation is so challenging today.

The apocalyptic sections of the Bible were not meant to be obscure, nor were they intended to breed unhealthy curiosity and fear. They were given to encourage moral and spiritual vigilance. Prior to writing this chapter, I visited a local Christian bookstore and viewed the shelf labeled "Prophecy." I counted nearly twenty books, most of them published within the past five years, which featured dramatic and scary titles about Armageddon and the Apocalypse. The tribe of evangelical soothsayers seems to grow each year because our society craves and thrives on sensationalism, and the church shares in this fascination. Today the word *apocalypse* may be used more frequently by Hollywood scriptwriters than by preachers because the prophets of Tinseltown know how to capitalize on our obsession with melodrama.

The Master's Eyes

The context of the Apocalyptic Discourse in Luke 21 tells a lot about human nature. While the disciples were with Jesus in the temple in Jerusalem, Jesus was watching the people putting their gifts into the temple treasury. Seeing a poor widow put in two pennies, he commented to those around him, "...this poor widow has put in more than all the others. All these people gave their gifts out of their wealth, but she out of her poverty put in all she had to live on" (Luke 21: 3-4). No comment from the disciples – total silence on the topic. Rather, they began to discuss what really turned their heads: "...how the temple was adorned with beautiful stones and with gifts dedicated to God." Jesus saw the spiritual richness of a widow's poverty; the disciples saw the material wealth of gifts given without sacrifice.

We have the same tendency of seeing the wrong things as we look toward the future. We seize upon the sensational and the dramatic; Jesus wants us to see beneath the superficial to the deeper issues of "apocalypse"—God's purposes revealed. Many students of prophecy spend countless hours exploring Revelation, looking for clues that will unlock the mystery of the future. The key is seeing the book as the revelation of Jesus Christ, not a literal representation of the future. Revelation portrays Jesus as the glorious, triumphant, returning King for whom doxologies abound and expressions of worship are jubilant and frequent. Failure to see *him* as the dominant theme is failure to understand the book. Focusing on chronology and specific events leads to confusion, distraction, and division.

Continuing in Luke 21, we notice that Jesus' purpose was not to satisfy the disciples' curiosity by teaching them eschatology, but to exhort them about their response to an uncertain future. The disciples were to be preoccupied with present alertness and obedience, not with anxiety about future events. Before he ascended to heaven, the risen Christ was asked by his disciples, "Lord, are you at this time going to restore the kingdom to Israel?" Because they were still gripped by eschatology, he replied,

> *It is not for you to know the times or dates the Father has set by his own authority. But you will receive power when the Holy Spirit comes on you, and you will be my witnesses in Jerusalem, and in all Judea and Samaria, and to the end of the earth.* Acts 1:7-8

Jesus wants his people to concentrate on evangelism, not eschatology. He does not require us to figure out the mysteries of the future, but to work toward preparing ourselves and others for that future. William Barclay aptly comments:

> *Jesus says that He does not know the day or the hour when He will come again. There were things which even He left without questioning in the hand of God. There can be no greater warning and rebuke to those who work out dates and timetables as to when He will come again. Surely it is nothing less than blasphemy for us to enquire into that of which our Lord consented to be ignorant.*[20]

Perhaps you have been a student of prophecy or have sat under the preaching or teaching of someone interested in eschatology. You may already have a locked-in belief of how the events will proceed. And you may be right! I will not try to alter your views on prophecy. What I do request, however, is that you put your eschatology into storage for the time being while we look into the Apocalyptic Discourse and discover ways to become a better disciple.

The Temple of the Lord

The disciples were moved with awe and wonder as they viewed the magnificent architecture and ornate decorations of the temple compound. Most of them were country boys, from up north in rural Galilee. They were ooh-ing and ahh-ing over the big-city sights, much like my friend Russell from Minnesota did when he first visited New York City.

And the Jerusalem temple was magnificent! Built between 20 B.C. and A.D. 35, Herod's temple covered one-sixth of old Jerusalem. Some of the stones were forty feet long, twelve feet high, and eighteen feet wide, and they were laid in an intricate pattern to show off their red and white coloring. This was the same temple where Jesus was circumcised on his eighth day; where twelve years later he first confounded the scribes; where Satan took him to tempt him to jump off its pinnacle; where he chased out the merchants, calling it a den of robbers instead of a house of prayer, and where very recently he had silenced his opponents.

Now, in a most solemn and emphatic way as the disciples were admiring it, Jesus predicted the temple's destruction—a total devastation, as indicated by Jesus' use of a double negative in Luke 21:6, better translated as "Not one stone will be left upon another which will not be torn down." Then Luke records, "'Teacher,' they asked, 'when will these things happen? And what will be the sign that they are about to take place?'" (v.7). (Matthew and Mark indicate that the questioning took place after they crossed the Kidron Valley and were on the Mount of Olives.)

Notice that the disciples were really asking *two* questions. Matthew reports the two questions more specifically: "Tell us, when will these things be, and what will be the sign of Your coming, and of the end of the age?" (Matt. 24:3 NASB). The disciples thought they were asking only one question, for surely, as foretold by the prophets, the destruction of the temple would usher in the Day of the Lord and the return of the Messiah. Luke's account does not show as clearly as Matthew's and Mark's that Jesus distinguished between the two questions, but a comparison of the parallel passages would show this to be the correct understanding of his response. It is not necessary to get bogged down in verse-by-verse exegesis to see that Jesus used the questions as a starting point for a teaching on alertness.

Five Warnings

In both eras, their own generation and the end time, disciples of Jesus must be watchful even while busily serving Christ. In verses 8-19 Jesus gives five statements about future events, each of which contains a warning.

"Many Will Come in My Name"

First, disciples are not to be misled by false messiahs (v.8). Jesus knew that the stresses of life and human impatience would cause people to latch on to deceivers who would claim "I am he." Gamaliel, "a teacher of the law," would later remind the Sanhedrin about two such men: Theudas, who drew four hundred followers, and Judas of Galilee, who led a band of revolutionaries (Acts 5:36-37). People of Samaria called Simon Magus "the Great Power" because of his wizardry (Acts 8:9-11). Not only Jews and Samaritans were waiting for a deliverer; the Romans, too, were expecting one. Seneca said that all men were look *ad salutem* ("to a savior"). The times were indeed ripe for false messiahs.

In our day we have seen several religious figures make messianic claims. Sun Myung Moon (died September 3, 2012), founder of the Unification Church, claimed himself to be "humanity's savior;" his "Moonies" teach that he is the most recent incarnation of the Messiah. Most new religions crown a new messianic leader or prophet, whether it be Maharishi Mahesh Yogi, Joseph Smith, or a New Age elephant. Desperate people are so gullible that they make bizarre commitments to whomever or whatever will promise comfort and security.

Jesus told his disciples that they must first be strong in their own knowledge of who he is, so that when false prophets and deliverers appear, they will not be misled. We, too, need to be convinced that Jesus is the *only* Messiah, for there is no other way to know God. Jesus could not have made it any clearer: "... if you do not believe that I am the one I claim to be, you will indeed die in your sins" (John 8:24). The smorgasbord approach to religion, which allows you to choose what pleases your individual taste, will probably continue to permeate our society, but Christians must believe that Jesus Christ is exclusive, not one of several possible alternatives. Modern man does not like such limitations, but God, not man, sets the rules.

"Do Not Be Frightened"

Second, Jesus told the disciples not to be frightened by wars, revolutions, or natural disasters (vv. 9-11). These are not signs of the end times (Mark 13: 7-8), but merely the beginning of birth pangs. Political and cosmic upheavals have always been with us, and though they are frightening, they are only evidences that things are not right as they are. Paul tells us that "the whole creation has been groaning as in the pains of childbirth" and with us eagerly awaits redemption (Romans 8:22-23).

Such disturbances were occurring in abundance in the first century. The Parthians were harassing the Romans; there were earthquakes in Laodicea and Pompeii; there was famine under

Claudius. Every century has had similar shocks, but the heavy labor that will give birth to the *Parousia,* the coming of Christ, is yet ahead. Disciples should not lose their composure during catastrophic times. Let the world panic, but God's people are to patiently trust in the Lord to deliver them.

"They Will Lay Hands on You"

Third, Jesus told his disciples not to be caught off guard by persecutions coming from established leaders (vv. 12-13). From the very beginning, he made it plain to all who followed him that persecution is part of discipleship. (See for example Matthew 5:10-12.) Notice that he tells them that religious and civil authorities will be the persecutors. The disciples will be treated as outlaws, but they must stand firm. God will give them wisdom when they are called to testify for Jesus before kings and governors.

In many countries of the world, Christians face this very situation today. Far from being commended for their piety, Christians are sometimes viewed as enemies of the state and are persecuted by the guardians of the law. The day may not be far off when Christians in America will likewise be oppressed. Many who oppose abortion feel constrained to break the law to act on their convictions, and suffer the consequences of fines, imprisonment, or both. Regardless of how we may feel about that, other issues will arise that will demand Christian activism and even civil disobedience.

There are times when Christians must actively defy a godless culture and state. Christians living in Nazi Germany, who passively watched as the Third Reich slaughtered millions of Jews and other innocent people, surely were not standing for Christ. Such a situation

> There are times when Christians must actively defy a godless culture and state.

233

may seem remote from our life in "Christian" America, but we need to ask what direction our society is headed, and prepare to be faithful when persecution comes.

"Do Not Worry Beforehand"

Fourth, Jesus told his disciples not to be anxious about what to say when they are called to stand before the courts, for he promised to give them wisdom and utterance that could not be refuted. Mark's account says, "Just say whatever is given you at the time, for it is not you speaking, but the Holy Spirit" (Mark 13:11b). Just as God had given words to Moses (Exodus 4:12) and to Jeremiah (Jeremiah 1:9) in the courts of Egypt and Judah, respectively, so he would do again for his people. And so he did. Stephen, Peter, Paul, and scores of Christian martyrs testified with such boldness and wisdom that it seemed as if the judges themselves were on trial.

Some Christians have abused this promise, taking it out of context and applying it to any ministry situation. Well-meaning preachers sometimes decide not to prepare their sermons so that God could speak through them unhindered by notes. One Christian in litigation over real estate even went to court without professional legal counsel, expecting God to be the defense. Notice two ideas in the text: Jesus is not prohibiting thought, but anxiety, or "worry beforehand" – and the promise is given for the specific purpose of defense when a disciple is on trial for his faith. In other cases, preparation, not spontaneity, is the way of the Lord.

"You Will Be Betrayed"

Fifth, Jesus said not to be surprised by hatred and rejection from their loved ones (vv. 16-19). Perhaps the toughest thing about the gospel is that at times it divides families. No one wants to be alienated from family members, but when the choice comes down to loyalty to Christ *or* peace in the family, a disciple must

234

choose the former. Jesus warned that the disciples would be betrayed "by parents, brothers, relatives and friends," and that "all men will hate you because of me." Those last three words are very important. I have met Christians who, by their ill-conceived and exuberant manner of witnessing, have seriously antagonized nonbelievers. The hostility is not about Christ, but about the inconsiderate way his gospel is presented by a self-righteous convert. The apostle Peter made it clear that not all suffering that Christians endure stems from their right conduct (I Peter 4:15).

As disciples, we need to understand why our witness may evoke a negative response, even in family members. The gospel is a rock. Some stumble on it; others build upon it. In some it inspires violent reaction; in others, it inspires belief. Because the gospel makes moral demands, no one can be passive about it. We are all under its judgment, and we must choose either to reject its authority or submit to it. Those who submit must not be surprised when others reject *us* along with the gospel.

Obeying Jesus' five negative commands is imperative for disciples, but compliance is easier if we are hopeful and alert. He says we must:

- not be misled by false messiahs
- not be frightened by wars or natural disasters
- not be caught off guard by persecution
- not be anxious about what to say
- not be surprised at rejection by loved ones

On a more positive note, he adds, "By standing firm, you will save yourselves" (v. 19).

Imminent Trouble

Thus far, the disciples have received little comfort from Jesus' words about the future. To their question about when the temple would be destroyed, Jesus said that it would occur in their generation. He warned them to flee to the mountains when they saw Jerusalem being besieged. In this time of punishment, wrath, and distress, some people would be slain by the sword and others would be disbursed as prisoners. Jerusalem would be thoroughly trampled.

This prophecy of horror came true with a vengeance. The Jewish historian Josephus tells of the grisly details that began in A.D. 70 when the armies of Titus, later to become emperor of Rome, laid siege to Jerusalem. Disease, starvation, and slaughter claimed 1,100,000 while 97,000 were deported as captives. Tales of ghoulish plundering, cannibalism, and diets of dung reveal how extreme the situation became. No wonder Jesus spoke with such passion as he urged his followers to flee Jerusalem. Many of the Christians took his advice, fled to the hills, and were saved.

Ultimate Triumph

The parallels of Luke 21:25-28 in Matthew and Mark imply that the next events that Jesus described would take place in a different era: They answer the question of when he would return and the end of the age. Mark's account begins: *But in those days* – words that the Jews would easily identify with the Old Testament concept of the "Day of the Lord." Three things will then occur: great cosmic upheaval (the sun and moon will be darkened, stars will fall, and the heavenly bodies will be shaken), people "will see the Son of Man coming in clouds," and "he will send his angels and gather his elect" (Mark 13:24-28).

The phrase *these things* in Mark 13: 29-30 refers to the earlier events, which the disciples could surely see coming as easily as they could predict the coming of summer by the sprouting of the leaves of a fig tree. When they saw *these things*, they would know that "it"—the time of great trouble—was right at the door. But no one knows the actual timing of "that day or hour," i.e., his return, not even the angels or Jesus himself, but only the Father.

The triumph of Jesus has already been attained: He has provided a satisfactory sacrifice for our salvation by his crucifixion, and he has victoriously conquered death by his resurrection. The war has been won, but his triumphal march will not occur until his return. As his disciples, we eagerly await that moment. We want to see him vindicated in the sight of both believers and scoffers. We long to see every knee bow before him and to hear every tongue confess his lordship. But, in the meantime, we had better pay heed to the strong words he gave his followers about remaining alert.

Watch and Work!

Despite all the information about the future given by Jesus in Apocalyptic Discourse, his main theme is a command for Christians to be watchful. Because Jesus was more concerned about giving exhortation than information, he was very emphatic about this: "Watch out...keep watch...be ready" (Matthew 24:4, 42, 44). Mark's Gospel uses similar working: "Watch out... So be on your guard...Be alert!...keep watch...Watch!" (Mark 13:5, 23, 33, 35, 37). The parallel verses in Luke 21 record the warnings as: "Watch out...Be careful...Be always on the watch" (vv. 8, 34, 36).

What does it mean for modern disciples to be watchful and alert? To simply sit on the sidelines, ready for anything? No, it certainly does not mean that we should be idle or passive. Paul admonished the Thessalonians about this. Apparently some were convinced that Jesus would return very soon, so they stopped working. The apostle warned them that they must follow his example and continue their labors so they "would not be a burden" to anyone (2 Thessalonians 3:7-8).

Jesus himself told us how he expects his people to be watchful: "Who then is the faithful and wise servant, whom the master has put in charge of the servants in his household to give them their food at the proper time? It will be good for that servant whose master finds him doing so when he returns" (Matthew 24: 45-46). In Mark's Gospel, Jesus expands on the concept by suggesting that one of the servants would be assigned to keep watch at the door: "...because you do not know when the owner of the house will come back...If he comes suddenly, don't let him find you sleeping. What I say to you, I say to everyone: "Watch!'" (Mark 13:35-37).

Just what is it, then, that we are to be doing in our alertness? Jesus wants us to be *working*—to be making disciples by witnessing in his name.

Over nineteen hundred years have passed since "these things" occurred, and we still do not know how many more years there will be before "those days." Yet many people scoff at the idea that Jesus will return, or believing that his promise to return must be understood metaphorically, or that perhaps he has already returned in his body, the church. Peter warned that "...in the last days scoffers will come [saying], 'Where is this "coming" he promised? Ever since our fathers died, everything goes on as it has since the beginning of creation.'" (2 Peter 3: 3-4).

Peter then gave three facts that scoffers do not consider:

1. Everything has *not* been the same since the beginning of creation; God has already judged the world once (the great flood).
2. God does not live by man's calendar; one day with him is like a thousand earth years, and vice versa.
3. God is patient, not wanting people to perish, but to repent.

The last idea comes from Jesus' words in Matthew's account of the Apocalyptic Discourse: "And this gospel of the kingdom will be preached in the whole world as a testimony to all nations, and then the end will come" (Matthew 24:14).

Scoffers fail to understand that God has a plan, which he has been implementing from the beginning of time, and global evangelization is a big part of it. Scoffers are going to be overtaken by the return of Jesus just like Noah's neighbors were overtaken by the flood (see Matthew 24:36-39; 2 Peter 3: 5-6). Believers should take no pleasure in that thought. Rather, living as alert disciples means warning the scoffers, convincing them of the reality of God's plan, encouraging them to repent, and teaching them to be disciples of Jesus Christ—all the while we are expecting his return.

"His last command—our first concern" is the motto of a great missionary church in Pennsylvania. And so it should be for all disciples of Jesus Christ. That last command was the Great Commission: "Therefore go and make disciples of all nations, baptizing them in the name of the Father and of the Son and of the Holy Spirit, and teaching them to obey everything I have commanded you. And surely I will be with you always, to the end of the age" (Matthew 28:19-20).

Discipleship Principle #14: Working Expectantly

As twentieth-century disciples of Jesus Christ, we surely must make his last command our first concern. It teaches us to keep our eyes on his coming even as we make disciples of the nations. As we do, we are abiding by Discipleship Principle # 14.

Discipleship Principle #14
Every day is lived and worked with a sense of anticipation and alertness by disciples because they expect that their Lord may return at any moment.

Chapter 15

ACHIEVING GREATNESS: SERVANTHOOD

Luke 22:24-30

Discipleship Principle # 15
Leadership in the kingdom of God is not attained through professional status, economic success, or natural ability, but through the exercise of a humble, selfless spirit of servanthood.

Can you imagine being a camp counselor for a dozen robust, adolescent boys? For three years, without a break? Or how would you like to be squad leader for a group of virile young men, all competing for the highest awards during a three-year Boy Scout Jamboree? It couldn't have been a whole lot different for Jesus.

We tend to think of Jesus' twelve disciples as a band of contented aesthetically and religiously oriented choir boys, romping the hills of Galilee and occasionally going to the big city—all the while overflowing with a spirit of peace, harmony, and mutual love and admiration. It wasn't that way at all! On at least three occasions, arguments broke out among the Twelve about who was the greatest. Since this was a recurring topic, this issue was probably always just beneath the surface.

The Social Staircase

Here are some terms that may evoke strong emotions in you: rivalry, competition, comparison, first place, champion, assertiveness. How you feel about those words most likely depends on your self-image. If you see yourself as a winner, you probably admire the qualities they represent. They might make you feel proud, satisfied, a bit superior if you're convinced that rugged individualism, survival of the fittest, and self-determination are important virtues and necessary components of all achievers. If you see yourself as a runner-up, or a loser, such words may make you feel threatened, inferior, and exposed. You feel cheated, ill-equipped to succeed in life like the winners do. You might also feel resentful of society's cruel system of rewarding the powerful with even more wealth, prestige, and power at the expense of the little people in society.

The technical phrase for this phenomenon is social stratification, a stacking process that ranks us according to predetermined standards. The word *stratification* comes from the field of geology, where it refers to layers of rock formations. Social stratification is seen in nearly every area of life. Some countries openly and unashamedly support a caste structure, a cultural ladder system whereby all citizens know exactly where they are slotted with regard to social class. Big business is stratified according to organizational charts and job descriptions, and politics is stratified according to constitutional and/or party lines. Perhaps the most obvious example of a stratification is the military, where there is a pecking order symbolized by the insignia worn on the lapel or sleeve.

Servant-Leaders

Anyone can be a leader in the kingdom. My mentor in ministry, Dr. Paul Bubna, defines a leader as someone who sees the goal and helps the group move toward it. Whether one is an executive, a secretary, a salesman, a middle manager, or a custodian, it matters not. Leadership is demonstrated whenever vision and vigor are employed in helping others succeed in accomplishing group objectives. A few corollaries follow from this definition of leadership. We are talking especially about kingdom leadership, but many successful business-people have found these principles effective in the secular marketplace as well.

First, we must reprogram our minds to the realization that kingdom leaders are servants to those they lead. Effective spiritual leaders are able to assume large amounts of responsibility because they embody kingdom qualities. They lead from the power of example, not the power of authority. Their followers are devoted volunteers, not conscripted and salaried clock-watchers. The reason they inspire such devotion and commitment is that their cause is noble and gripping. People willingly follow leaders who give them something worth living and dying for and whose own lives reflect a mutuality of interest.

When Jesus told his disciples that to be truly great they would need to be childlike, he was giving them some important clues about leadership. Children are teachable, not rigid; trusting, not suspicious; eager to please, not self-absorbed; openly dependent, not self-sufficient. These gracious qualities are essential in servant-leaders. They boil down to three L's: Leaders are learners, leaners, and lovers. They have a right perspective on their mission, their own limitations, and the needs of their followers.

Following from this is a corollary: Kingdom leaders consider those they lead to be more important than themselves. Jesus communicated this dramatically when, knowing "that the Father had put all things under his power, and that he had come from God and was returning to God...he got up from the meal, took off his outer clothing, and wrapped a towel around his waist. After that, he poured water into a basin and began to wash his disciples' feet, drying them with the towel that was wrapped around him" (John 13:3-5).

Imagine that! Knowing that he was in control of the situation, Jesus took the lowly position of a slave to show honor to his followers. He certainly wanted to set an example for them, but he also wanted them to know how much he valued them. Good leaders consider their followers to be of highest importance because, in fact, they are.

The practical consequence of this truth is another principle: Kingdom leaders use work to get people done, rather than using people to get work done. In the world, people are workers, part of the machinery to produce the finished goods. In the kingdom of God, people are the goods being prepared for glory. Jesus died for people, not for a program, a project, or a profit margin.

You can be sure that a ministry, whether church or parachurch, is not of the kingdom when the work "out there" is more important than the people "in here." Observing how a leader treats his or her support staff will tell you a lot about how close that ministry is to the kingdom. The most obvious but least-credited support staff for any leader is found at home, yet many "great leaders" have sacrificed the neglected, wounded, and abused children of leaders in the church. On the other hand, I have also observed with much admiration men who very easily could have gained renown as Christian celebrities, but they shunned the limelight for the more worthy goal of serving their families.

Disputing Disciples

Jesus used several events to address the issue of social stratification. One episode occurred shortly after his transfiguration and was reported in Matthew 18, Mark 9, and Luke 9, where we learn that "an argument started among the disciples as to which of them would be the greatest" (Luke 9:46). Undoubtedly the events surrounding the transfiguration played into this situation. The privileged status of Peter, James, and John, who were chosen to go up the mountain with Jesus, may have been resented by the other nine. Their imaginations probably ran wild as they wondered what they had missed, and no doubt Peter wasn't too quick to tell them how he had put his foot into his mouth with his suggestion of three tabernacles. Nor of the rebuke that came out of the sky.

To make matters worse, when Jesus and the three came down from the mount, the other nine were in a most embarrassing situation. A father had brought his demonized son to the disciples, asking them to free him from the demon.

> In the midst of their shame, they were dreaming of fame.
> Very human, these twelve.

Unfortunately, they failed, and were humiliated as it happened in front of a crowd. Jesus expelled the demon from the young man and then chastised the disciples for their lack of faith.

It was against this backdrop that the argument arose about who was greatest. Amazing! In the midst of their shame, they were dreaming of fame. Very human – these twelve. Imagine their chagrin when Jesus, putting his arm around a little child, said, "...unless you change and become like little children, you will never enter the kingdom of heaven. Therefore, whoever humbles himself like this child is the greatest in the kingdom of heaven" (Matthew 18:304; cf. Luke 9:48).

Another time, not too long after the previous incident, James and John implored Jesus to give them the places of honor at his right and left in his kingdom. Matthew reports that their mother made the request, but either way, "When the ten heard about this, they became indignant with James and John" (Mark 10:41; cf. Matthew 20:24). Again, the context reveals how inappropriate the request was. Jesus had just told his disciples what was going to happen in Jerusalem: he would be betrayed to the Jewish leaders and executed by the Romans. Rather than being overcome by grief for him, James and John were thinking only about themselves and wanted assurance that they would be honored in his glory. At least it was somewhat to their credit that they *did* believe in his kingdom! To defuse this volatile situation, Jesus gave the Twelve a short lecture on kingdom leadership, repeating that greatness is directly related to service, not status, to responsibility, not privilege: "For even the Son of Man did not come to be served, but to serve, and to give his life as ransom for many" (Mark 10:45).

The third eruption occurred at the Last Supper, again a very untimely moment for an argument about who was the greatest. It was an incredible occasion for discord to break out—the night of the Passover celebration. Knowing this would be his last evening meal with his friends and that the next day he would be executed, Jesus wanted this Passover to be very special, an opportunity to link the old and new covenants in a holy meal. His plans started out working quite well. First, as Jesus had told them, two of the disciples found the man carrying a pitcher of water and were led to the room to prepare the meal. Next, during the traditional celebration of Israel's escape from Egypt, Jesus used one of the traditional four cups of wine to symbolize his blood, and passed around the bread as a symbol of his broken body. Then he gently but definitively predicted that one of the men at the table would be his betrayer. In that setting *a dispute rose among them as to which of them was considered to be greatest* (Luke 22:24).

Isn't it amazing that Jesus used even this moment of sacred and solemn significance to gently give another lesson on discipleship! Why was he so patient? Before we become too condemning of the selfish ambition of the Twelve, let us notice a few facts. First, Jesus had handpicked these men because he knew they would be achievers, willing to risk everything and live for ideals greater than the prevailing socio-religious culture all around them. Jesus could see certain admirable traits in these potential leaders: commitment, pursuit of success, aggressive and competitive instincts. But they needed to be rechanneled into kingdom qualities.

Furthermore, notice that Jesus did not roundly condemn their desire to be great. In fact, he went on to promise them a special role in his kingdom (cf. vv.28-30). Instead of trying to dilute their drive for significance, he gave them a new outlook on greatness and on leadership.

Spiritual Stratification

From these occasions when Jesus spoke to his immediate followers about kingdom leadership, greatness, and servanthood, there are several observations we might make about spiritual stratification, particularly as it applies to discipleship.

The first important lesson is: *self-seeking blinds us to the sacred*. We have an amazing lack of ability to recognize sacred moments. Little did the disciples realize that they were on most holy ground in the upper room and experiencing perhaps the most holy moment of all history. The Last Supper would become an event celebrated for hundreds of years by other disciples. The Twelve were witnessing a hint of eternity, a foreshadowing of the great banquet feast in the messianic kingdom. And yet there they were, arguing about which of them was the greatest.

Picture in your mind what was happening. Jesus had said, "One of you is going to betray me." No doubt they started looking at each other for clues to the traitor's identity. There sits Simon the Zealot—discouraged because Jesus isn't using his power to overthrow the Romans. That's Simon in a nutshell! When he sees the eyes on him, he probably says to himself, "I bet it's Matthew. Who can trust someone who sold out to the Roman government like Matthew, the tax-collector, did?" Matthew looks at Thomas and thinks, "I know all about him. Since he's not even sure that Jesus is who he says he is, he could be the traitor." Thomas looks at John: "Look at him over there, leaning on the Master. So close and cozy. I bet it's all a sham." And John, perhaps, looks at Judas and thinks, "I bet it's Judas. I think he's been stealing shekels from the common purse." But no one was sure, so a dispute broke out over a related matter. Who is the greatest? Who is the betrayer? A very human kind of concern.

Don't fail to miss the tragic irony about this—it says something quite true about human nature. Rather than reaching out to Jesus with loving concern that he would be betrayed, the disciples went inward and focused on themselves. We humans are capable of heroic deeds, but heroism and courage demand that we overcome our selfish preoccupation. Only Jesus was truly "the man for others." Perhaps one of the reasons for Christianity's memorial meal is to force us to sit down in a sacred moment and reflect on the Lord's death, forgetting our self-seeking impulses. In a sense the Lord's Supper should be an unnecessary institution. We should be able to have many such holy occasions, an ongoing sense of God's presence. We should celebrate the death of our Lord Jesus Christ in many ordinary, secular moments of life. But we don't do that, for the most part because we are blinded to the sacred by our egocentrism.

What was Jesus' response to this nearly blasphemous activity going on at the Last Supper? We might have expected a harsh rebuke. "What is wrong with you guys? Don't you understand what's going on? I'm going to die tomorrow. This bread and wine are my body and blood, here today but gone tomorrow! I want you to remember me this way. This is a sacred hour." But, instead, there was a gentle reminder: "My friends, you are acting like mere worldlings. In the heathen nations, rulers abuse their authority, wanting to be called the greatest. It must not be this way with you." Jesus patiently gave them a lesson in humility and servanthood, which he had visually demonstrated by ungirding himself, going to each one, and washing their feet (John 13:1-17). Then he affirmed them: "You have stood by me in my trials. When I am at my banquet table in the kingdom, you will sit and eat and drink with me. In fact, you will be the leaders; you will be the judges of the twelve tribes of Israel"

(Luke 22:28-30, paraphrased). The response of Jesus to his disciples' selfish striving was so incredible that perhaps they finally learned this lesson about leadership and also would be more sensitive to sacred moments in the future.

A second insight gained from this incident is: *Serving others is not to be viewed as a stepping-stone to greater power and position.* Jesus was not saying that if his followers wished to rise to great heights in the church, they must first prove themselves in a lowly place. Not at all. That principle is used effectively in the world, but it reflects an improper attitude because it caters to selfish ambition. Jesus was saying that faithful service in a lowly place is itself true greatness. Stepping-stone service is out of step with our Lord. Likewise, if we refuse to allow others to serve us, it is likely that we are rendering our own service with a wrong motivation. Kingdom living requires that service be given and accepted with a noncompetitive spirit. Self-advancement must never be its goal.

Think of Peter's response to the foot-washing incident: "Lord, are you going to wash my feet? ... No, you shall never wash my feet" (John 13:6, 8). This falls into the category of prideful one-upmanship. Humility is a necessary element of spiritual leadership, and receiving someone else's service can be more humbling than rendering service ourselves. Whether serving or being served, our motive should never be "What's in it for me?" True servanthood is an act of love that is totally devoid of selfish striving toward personal goals. We are to allow that love to flow freely in either direction.

A third observation is this: *Leadership in the kingdom is fundamentally and qualitatively different from leadership in the world.* For several reasons. First, leadership positions in the kingdom are based upon derived authority. There is only one head to the body of Christ, and all other members are subject to him. No one has authority in God's kingdom that does not come from the King. That authority is delegated only if it is spiritually authentic. We are but stewards, even of authority. In other words, leadership in the kingdom is never self-generated. The family of God has suffered much from self-anointed leaders. The shepherding movement, which was a form of spiritual stratification, put many earnest disciples under the authority of misguided and overly authoritarian leaders. A good check to this kind of abuse is for leaders to be chosen from the body so that all members have a say.

Sometimes this principle is ignored because the strong personality or charisma of a leader overwhelms the rest of the body. Paul Vitz, associate professor of psychology at New York University, quotes Wayne Jossee's review of a study of encounter groups at Stanford University:

> *Theoretical orientation" seemed to matter little, though "leader style" did. The more empathetic and supportive leaders ... achieved the greatest number of positive changes while the more aggressive and "charismatic" leaders were correlated with negative outcomes.*[21]

This finding certainly has significant implications in our selection of pastoral and other spiritual leaders. We need to be careful about too quickly following aggressive, verbally gifted personalities. The body should be encouraged to recognize those who are truly qualified and then provide opportunities for such individuals to serve in leadership positions. The key word, or course, is "serve."

This brings us to another way in which leadership in the kingdom differs from leadership in the world: *Kingdom leadership is granted only for the purpose of serving, not for personal aggrandizement.* Luke 22:26 makes that very clear: "...the greatest among you should be like the youngest, and the one who rules like the one who serves." We are given special responsibility, not special status, when we are called into leadership. The church needs responsible, hands-on leaders who are more interested in "server-ship" than in wielding their authority. Organizational flow charts in the business world show a powerful CEO at the top and then lines of decreasing status going to boxes showing vice-presidents and middle managers, down to the folks in the mailroom. God's kingdom flow chart is inverted. The real leader is the one who best serves the rest because he or she has accepted responsibility for their welfare.

Kingdom leadership also demands humility, a quality not often prized by the worldly. Those most humble are most qualified as leaders because they have the truest perspective on God's greatness and thus an accurate appraisal of themselves. This is not a denigration of our role as God's servants, for Christians are supposed to have a healthy sense of self-worth. But, though made in God's image, we are not to think of ourselves more highly than we ought, for we all have flaws and have sinned. Moses, who was a great leader, was also considered to be the meekest man on the face of the earth. The most effective religious leaders I've met are always a bit surprised that they were chosen to lead. But they, like the apostle Paul, base their ministry on "the meekness and gentleness of Christ" (2 Corinthians 10:1).

Level Living

One final observation about spiritual stratification as it applies to discipleship is this: Jesus did not intend to establish a new hierarchy by inverting the social ladder. He dismantled hierarchies altogether. He was not saying that the powerless, the socially disadvantaged, and the weak are now the real leaders, thereby leaving the wealthy, the powerful, and the privileged at the bottom of the ladder.

> Jesus did not intend to establish a new hierarchy by inverting the social ladder. He dismantled hierarchies altogether.

Instead, relationships in the kingdom are between brothers and sisters, not masters and slaves. This is why Paul was able to say in Galatians 3:28, There is neither Jew nor Greek, slave nor free, male nor female, for you are all one in Christ Jesus. Because in Christ we stand on level ground, "the one who is least in the kingdom of God is greater than John [the Baptist]," who was the greatest of all prophets (Luke 7:28). In the new economy of the kingdom, God regards all of his children as equally important — or as Francis Schaeffer says, "There are no little people" in the kingdom.

This is one reason why regular observance of the Lord's Supper is so important within the church body. Whenever we examine ourselves in light of Christ's sacrifice on our behalf, we are called to the cross and to the level living it implies. Calvary was a hill and the cross was its pinnacle, but the ground at the foot of that cross was level and still is, so all who are there are brothers and sisters. The Lord's Supper is an equalizer, a reminder that we are members of one flock led by one Shepherd who commands unity that does not allow for man-imposed distinctions.

Early in the history of Christianity, disharmony was a problem in Corinth because the class system characterizing Greek society had infiltrated the church. The apostle Paul chastised the Corinthians for allowing factions and divisions to weaken their fellowship and even to overshadow the significance of the sacramental meal:

"In the following directives I have no praise for you, for your meetings do more harm than good. In the first place, I hear that when you come together as a church, there are divisions among you. ... When you come together, it is not the Lord's Supper you eat, for as you eat, each of you goes ahead without waiting for anyone else. One remains hungry, another gets drunk. Don't you have homes to eat and drink in? Or do you despise the church of God and humiliate those who have nothing? ... Shall I praise you for this? Certainly not! ... anyone who eats and drinks without recognizing the body of the Lord eats and drinks judgment on himself" (1 Corinthians 11:17-18, 20-22, 29).

What was the problem in Corinth? Some people came to the Lord's Supper early because they were free to do so. They came to the table and gobbled down the food. Christian slaves, who did not live on their own time schedule, came when they could. Often they arrived when the food was gone and the wealthier people were half-drunk. But the Lord's Supper obliterates hierarchical distinctions. There is no pecking order in the kingdom of God. It is a family dedicated to serving God by serving each other.

Discipleship Principle #15: Achieving Greatness

"Corporate culture" is an important idea in the modern business world. Managers who want to create the best environment for work must learn the principle that people are more important than the products, projects, and even profit. Achieving the corporate culture of the kingdom of God is even more demanding of its leaders. Because the goals of the kingdom are eternal and so very special, greatness of leadership cannot be judged by the world's standards, which brings us to Discipleship Principle #15—which may be the most important one of all:

Discipleship Principle # 15
Leadership in the kingdom of God is not attained through professional status, economic success, or natural ability, but through the exercise of a humble, selfless spirit of servanthood.

ENDNOTES

1. David Mace, *How to Have a Happy Marriage*, quoted in Dick Walther, *TWR Leadership Ideas*, Issue #23 (January, 1988).
2. Willy Brandt, *North/South, A Programme for Survival* (London: Pan Books Ltd., 1980), p. 32.
3. Richard Foster, *Money, Sex & Power* (San Francisco: Harper and Row, 1985), pp. 102, 103.
4. Gene Edwards, *A Tale of Three Kings* (Augusta, ME: Christian Books, 1980).
5. Leon Morris, *The Gospel Accoridng to St. Luke* (Grand Rapids: William B. Eerdmans, 1974), p. 130.
6. Bill Gothard, *Instructions For Our Most Important Battle* (Oak Brook, IL: Institutes in Basic Youth Conflicts, 1976), pp. 9, 13.
7. Gothard, p. 9.
8. Dick Walther, "Power to Build People," in *TWR Leadership Ideas*, Issue #31 (July, 1988).
9. Andrew Weil, *The Natural Mind* (Boston: Houghton Mifflin, 1973), p. 32.
10. Henri Nouwen, *Reaching Out* (Glasgow: William Collins, 1976), p. 16.
11. T. W. Manson, *The Sayings of Jesus* (Grand Rapids: William B. Eerdmans, 1979), p. 72.

[12] Gordon MacDonald, *Ordering Your Private World* (Nashville: Oliver Nelson, 1984), p. 51ff.

[13] Larry Richards, *A Theology of Christian Education* (Grand Rapids: Zondervan, 1975), ch. 3.

[14] Larry Crabb, *Inside Out* (Colorado Springs: NavPress, 1988)

[15] John Howard Yoder, *The Politics of Jesus* (Grand Rapids: William B. Eerdmans, 1972), p. 65.

[16] IBID., p. 65

[17] William Barclay, *The First Three Gospels* (Philadelphia: The Westminster Press, 1966), pp. 145, 146.

[18] T. W. Manson, p. 290.

[19] John MacArthur, *The Master's Men* (Chicago: Moody Press, 1985), p. 24.

[20] William Barclay, *The Gospel of Mark in The Daily Study Bible* (Philadelphia: Westminster Press, 1954), p. 336.

[21] Paul Vitz quoting Wayne Jossee in *Psychology as Religion* (Herts., England: Lyon Publishing, 1979), p. 42.

CPSIA information can be obtained
at www.ICGtesting.com
Printed in the USA
FFHW021252141019
55565374-61364FF